TRIUMPH
B O O K S

ON THE CLOCK: TORONTO MAPLE LEAFS

ON THE CLOCK: TORONTO MAPLE LEAFS

Behind the Scenes with the Toronto Maple Leafs at the NHL Draft

SCOTT WHEELER

TRIUMPH
BOOKS

No part of this publication may be reproduced, stored in a retrieval system, or transmitted in any form by any means, electronic, mechanical, photocopying, or otherwise, without the prior written permission of the publisher, Triumph Books LLC, 814 North Franklin Street, Chicago, Illinois 60610.

Library of Congress Cataloging-in-Publication Data available upon request.

This book is available in quantity at special discounts for your group or organization. For further information, contact:

Triumph Books LLC
814 North Franklin Street
Chicago, Illinois 60610
(312) 337-0747
www.triumphbooks.com

Printed in U.S.A.
ISBN: 978-1-63727-119-3
Design by Preston Pisellini
Page production by Patricia Frey

For Madelyn Jane and Beaumont

CONTENTS

Foreword by Steve Dangle xi

Introduction xv

1 Jim Gregory's Draft Legacy 1

2 The First Pick 16

3 Bruce Boudreau, Randy Carlyle, and
a 1970s History of Coaches 35

4 From Amateur to Entry and "Big Daddy"
Bob McGill. 51

5 The Defections of the Ihnacak Brothers. 60

6 Toronto's First Draft...and First
No. 1 Pick 73

7 The Gord Stellick Years and the Belleville
Bulls Draft 85

8 From a Lost Draft Year to Developing
the Leafs' Lost Prospects. 102

9 A Blockbuster Trade's Forgotten Piece 115

10 The Latest Pick 131

11 The John Ferguson Jr. Era 146

12 The Luke Schenn Pick 165

13 How Tyler Biggs Led to Morgan Rielly
and William Nylander 181

14 Inside the 2016 Draft Lottery with Brendan
Shanahan 201

15 Jack Han and the Crossroads between
Drafting and Developing 213

16 The Pandemic Draft Kid 230

Acknowledgments 245

About the Author 251

FOREWORD

AFTER A LIFETIME of following the draft from home, the 2014 NHL Draft in Philadelphia was the first one I ever attended in person. The two things I remember the most perfectly encapsulate what it feels like to be a Leafs fan.

The first was on Day 1. The Leafs had the eighth overall selection that year. After years of drafting for size, there was a real thirst for some skill. I, along with many Leafs fans, wanted either Nikolaj Ehlers or a young, flashy Swede by the name of William Nylander.

When the Vancouver Canucks picked Jake Virtanen at sixth overall, it meant the Leafs would be able to grab one of those two. When the Carolina Hurricanes selected Hadyn Fleury No. 7 it meant the Leafs could get whichever one of those two they wanted. I was elated! I was thrilled! I was... terrified. What if they go off the board? What if they draft some big guy who can't skate?

The Leafs put my fears to bed when they picked Nylander eighth overall. From that moment on, everything would go perfectly smooth for Willy and the Leafs. At least, that's what I hoped at the time. I wasn't thinking about constant trade rumours and I certainly wasn't thinking about a several-months-long contract holdout. Every draft is built on hope.

My second memory came on Day 2. If you've ever been to a draft, you know Day 2 is hangover day. What I mean by that is everybody is hungover. There are fewer people there than on Day 1 and the ones who are there are a lot quieter than they were the night before.

In front of the stage where more than 200 young players are drafted into the league each year, right where there was an NHL ice surface just weeks prior, the draft floor is littered with dozens of tables featuring NHL GMs, coaches, scouts, and a handful of executives' kids running from table to table in a jersey that's at least two sizes too large for them.

During the fourth round of the draft, I got to hear those iconic words in person: "We have a trade to announce."

When that happens, the building goes silent. Fans from all over the league are in attendance and each and every one of them thinks their team is about to make either the smartest or dumbest deal in franchise history.

Then it was announced—the Toronto Maple Leafs have traded the 94th selection in the draft to the St. Louis Blues along with defenceman Carl Gunnarsson in exchange for defenceman Roman Polak.

After several moments of complete silence, one fan bellowed deep from their diaphragm, "That's a horrible trade!"

Absolutely every person in the building heard it, including every NHL executive on the draft floor, which included then Leafs general manager Dave Nonis.

Despite being completely different players, Nylander and Polak are kind of alike. Nylander has been polarizing with Leafs fans for being all skill and no work while Polak was seen as all work but no skill. Meanwhile, Polak was a key presence for the rebuilding Buds while Nylander has been a key piece coming out of said rebuild. Fans thought Nylander was a great pick and fans thought Nylander was a terrible pick. Fans thought Polak was a terrible pickup and fans thought Polak was a great pickup.

The point is, after the excitement of the draft, after every scribe has scribbled their last thought about some teenaged hockey player who could be the next big thing or the next big bust, the players must write their own story.

In the mid-2000s, I was completely jacked for a certain Leafs goalie prospect. Every time I watched him, nobody could beat him. From the moment I first saw him play, I knew I was watching someone special. I knew I was watching the Leafs' future in net.

That goalie was Tuukka Rask.

Your team can do everything right, scout every game, do every interview, run every background check, and have the player of their dreams fall to them in the draft, just to trade them away before they've even played their first game.

In November 2005, the Leafs traded tough guy Nathan Perrott to the Dallas Stars for a conditional sixth-round pick in 2006. The Leafs practically gave Perrott away. Who could have known the Leafs would use that pick on a man who would end up making an unlikely NHL All-Star appearance a decade later in 2016—none other than fan phenomenon Leo Komarov.

You just never know.

Even when you know, you never know. I went to the 2016 draft in Buffalo. The Leafs had the first overall pick for the first time since 1985. Even though there was a 99.99 percent chance the Leafs were drafting Auston Matthews first overall, my lungs refused to breathe a full breath of air until Leafs assistant general manager Mark Hunter announced the pick for the entire hockey world to hear. Only then would it be real.

With this book, Scott Wheeler will take you through the ins and outs, the ups and downs, as well as the known and unknown of the NHL draft with the Leafs. After reading, you'll have new reasons to hope, new reasons to dread, and every reason to think the National Hockey League is simultaneously being run by the smartest people on the planet and a bunch of confused golden retrievers just trying their best.

Now, allow Scott to take you on a journey behind the scenes with the Toronto Maple Leafs at the NHL draft.

Steve Dangle is a hockey YouTuber and the host of The Steve Dangle Podcast, *known for his videos about the Maple Leafs. He is the author of* This Team Is Ruining My Life (But I Love Them): How I Became a Professional Hockey Fan.

INTRODUCTION

I DON'T THINK I *really* understood what draft day meant to me until I was sitting on my couch in the East End of Toronto watching it play out in the NHL Network's studios in Secaucus, New Jersey, in October 2020. There was something about it that just felt off. Namely, we were in the middle of a pandemic. As I settled in, turned on the TV, rested my phone next to me, and began opening folders of notes on my laptop to prepare to write—which, on draft day, is an exercise in trying to keep up—I wasn't excited. The magic of the day, a day normally filled with it, felt distant.

In normal times, the week of the NHL draft is the biggest thrill of my year. I spend each preceding season travelling the hockey world to watch and learn about the sport's best young players, telling their stories from rinks and hotel rooms, and dissecting the ins and outs of their games (the oddity of which is not lost on me). When I'm not on the road, my days fill with video work, local junior and minor-pro games, and phone calls—*a lot* of phone calls. I write hundreds of thousands of words on every new draft class (enough to fill several books like this one), each of them in anticipation of two days in June. A few of the kids' stories always seem to leave a mark, too, so much so that by the time *their* big day arrives I'm anxious to see where they'll land—or whether they'll be picked at all.

Then it all culminates with the adrenaline rush of days that begin and end in the early morning in one of the NHL's cities.

When I'm in it, I try not to take it for granted. I try to live in the moment. To latch on to the overwhelming relief that follows after I hit send on my final piece on that year's draft class and alert my editor that it's ready. To tell myself that my preparedness paid off. To be thankful that this is my job.

Other journalists will tell you about those same feelings when the team they cover wins the Stanley Cup and they were among those who got to put history into words. I'm lucky enough to experience those feelings at the end of every year with my *thing*. The draft is my Stanley Cup.

But on the first Tuesday of October in 2020, it felt at first duller. I was meant to be in Montreal, sitting in a make-shift media riser typically installed at the rear of the lower bowl opposite the stage, surrounded by my colleagues, typing through every spare minute and running across the stands to speak with sources in all of the others. NHL scouts and general managers were meant to be intersecting on the draft floor, a buzz of uneasy parents, nervous players, and reassuring agents surrounding them. This time, though, in place of staging and handshakes and photo shoots, there was just me and my TV, and the players and theirs.

Maybe a little to my surprise, the feeling when I first sat down on my couch to watch it all unfold from afar didn't last. When the draft started, 217 kids still got to live out the best day of their young lives, and the many thousands of people who played a part in their stories got to share in that moment, in that success, with them. And it all mattered just the same to each of those involved in that orbit as it did to all those who'd been picked in the 57 NHL drafts before it.

While it may have felt different, there was still magic in the people and their stories. There was magic in the phone call I got the following morning from Michael Rossi, the father of Marco Rossi, who'd just become the ninth overall pick of the Minnesota Wild, thanking me for telling Marco's story. (Two years earlier, I'd moved in with Marco and his billet family for a weeklong stay for an immersive story, shortly after he'd moved from Austria to Canada to pursue his dream with the Ottawa 67's.) There was magic in the text I got from Mairri McConnell immediately after her son, Zayde Wisdom, whose against-all-odds story had left one of those indelible marks on me, was selected in the fourth round by the Philadelphia Flyers. "I was just speaking about you. You are a big part of this. Thank you so much," read her message. "Team Wisdom. I can assure you he will not let you down."

For Michael and Marco, and Mairri and Zayde, when the last names Rossi and Wisdom were called, there was no point of reference, no consideration for what another draft day could have looked like, because they hadn't lived any other. There was just their day, their story, and that magic.

In the weeks after their day, I began working on this book with them in mind. My only goal for the book became this:

find and tell more of those stories. The only requirement was that they each be about the Leafs in some way or another.

Part of that equation comes easy. I'm from here. I was born and raised in Aurora, one of the city's suburbs. Before moving back to nearby Newmarket to be closer to family in the winter of 2022, I called Toronto home for five years. My son, Beaumont, was born in the city's east end, at Michael Garron Hospital, in the midst of my authoring this book. He has Toronto on his birth certificate. I know this place and I grew up on its team. Before reporting on the draft was my *thing*, reporting on the Leafs was.

Part of that equation is harder to solve, though. Because there may not be a team in pro sports whose stories have been chronicled as thoroughly as the Leafs' have. Because telling someone else's story takes trust, and patience, and a craft that I will work my entire life trying to hone and will never perfect.

In the pages that follow, I've endeavoured to go behind the scenes with the people who are at the centre of the big stories—the picks, the trades, the moments—while discovering and telling new ones you've never heard along the way.

You'll hear from David Gregory, Walt McKechnie, Bruce Boudreau, Randy Carlyle, Bob McGill, Peter Ihnacak, Wendel Clark, Gord Stellick, Scott Thornton, Steve Bancroft, Danny Flynn, Drake Berehowsky, Todd Warriner, Staffan Kronwall, John Ferguson Jr., Luke Schenn, Dave Poulin, Chris Bergeron, Rico Blasi, Brendan Shanahan, Jack Han, and Ryan and Todd Tverberg. And you'll read about many more.

I hope you'll find the same magic in these stories as I did writing them and as my subjects did living them.

ON THE CLOCK: TORONTO MAPLE LEAFS

1

JIM GREGORY'S DRAFT LEGACY

ONE OF DAVID GREGORY'S earliest memories is of the day his dad, Jim, became the general manager of the Maple Leafs. It was the fall of 1969, and David was starting third grade at St. Richard Catholic School in Scarborough, Ontario, when his teacher pulled him aside to ask him about it—and, in turn, explain it to him.

More than five decades after that moment, hockey fans are most likely to recognize Jim's name for his role as the man who for decades stepped up to podiums as the master of ceremony for Day 2 of the NHL Entry Draft.

But there is no history of the NHL draft, nor of the Leafs, without him. Jim's legacy *is* the draft, and his hockey story started in Toronto before it ever existed.

The inaugural NHL draft (at first known as the NHL Amateur Draft) didn't take place until 1963, nearly 60 years into the league's life. For much of the first half of the NHL's history to date, the league's Original Six teams developed most of their would-be players themselves, often owning, operating, and sponsoring the junior hockey clubs that fed into the NHL.

In 1952, when a 17-year-old Jim moved from Dunville, Ontario, to Toronto to attend St. Michael's College School, the Leafs sponsored two teams, the St. Michael's Majors and the Toronto Marlborough Athletic Club, commonly known as the Marlboros, which both played in the Ontario Hockey Association (OHA).

Jim hoped to make the Majors' Junior B team. When he was cut by the team, Father David Bauer, the school's legendary teacher, hockey coach, and manager, prodded him to help out with the Junior A club as a trainer and stat keeper. Within a few years of his graduation from the school, Jim had become the Majors' everyman, all but operating the team on his own on a $68-per-week salary. Father Bauer had become his biggest mentor in life. In 1959, Bauer leveraged his NHL connections to get Jim an interview with Leafs owner Stafford Smythe, an interview that led to his hiring as a part-time scout for the Leafs and summer employee at the Smythe family's sand and gravel pits, roles he had to fill alongside his jobs with the Majors.

Two years later, in 1961, Jim was serving as general manager of the Majors within the Leafs' farm system, and they won the Memorial Cup under his guidance.

A season after that Memorial Cup win, when the Majors withdrew from the OHA's top junior league due to the impact its busy schedule was having on the athletes' academic performance, Jim and many of his players were moved to the

Toronto Neil McNeil High School Maroons for a single season in the Metro Junior A League. There, as head coach and general manager, Jim led the Maroons to a league championship and the finals of the J. Ross Robertson Cup (a trophy still handed out in today's Ontario Hockey League). In 1963, when the Maroons were amalgamated with the Marlboros to stabilize the Leafs' farm system, Jim was retained as head coach once more, guiding the Marlboros to his second Memorial Cup in his first season with his new team and a third in 1967 as the team's general manager.

So by the time Jim was named Maple Leafs general manager for the 1968–69 season, he had already shaped the generation of hockey players he was taking over leadership of. Though he was just 33 years old and the league's youngest general manager, Jim had helped develop future NHL players like Gerry Cheevers, Gary Smith, Pete Stemkowski, Ron Ellis, Gerry Meehan, and Mike Corrigan, among others, with the Majors, Maroons, and Marlboros.

Among Jim's first orders of business when Smythe and co-owner Harold Ballard promoted him from assistant general manager to general manager to replace the fired Punch Imlach was to build the team's first dedicated scouting department, hiring five full-time scouts. Throughout his tenure, he also paved the way for new avenues for NHL clubs to find and sign players, becoming one of the first general managers to recruit out of Europe when he signed Borje Salming and Inge Hammarstrom in 1973.

With his dad in charge of the team, David grew up inside Maple Leaf Gardens. On Saturdays, he would attend the morning skates, watch the early-afternoon Marlies game, and then hang around so that he could watch the Leafs game that night. Players and staff on the Marlies and Leafs became his heroes. In days spent at the rink, David watched as Jim shaped the way a modern hockey team should draft and build, milling about as his dad worked through problems with coaches King Clancy and John McLellan or lead scout Bob Davidson.

Whenever Jim wasn't on the road with the team and David would return from school to their Scarborough home to find his dad on the phone in the kitchen, he would pull up a chair and listen to his dad talk to the team's coach or opposing general managers.

By the time David was a high school student at Brebeuf College School, he'd also grown old enough to know that his dad wasn't going to be general manager of the Leafs forever, and his fandom of the team changed, with each passing season taking on even more meaning than the last. Though Jim guided the team out of late 1960s struggles to eight playoff appearances in 10 years, drafting stars like Darryl Sittler and Lanny McDonald, by the late 1970s the Gregory family knew that he'd reached a point in his tenure where the success of the team was directly intertwined with their patriarch's livelihood.

When the Leafs lost the first two games of their 1978 quarterfinal series against the Islanders, David vividly remembers his mother Rosalie's constant anxiety. When the Leafs forced a Game 7 and the Gregorys gathered at their grandparents' house to watch it as a family, Rosalie was so visibly on edge and nervous that David asked her if she was all right.

"If the Leafs don't win this series, I think your dad will get fired," she said.

"Oh boy," David answered.

Though the Leafs won the series with a thrilling 2–1 overtime win in that Game 7 and Jim kept his job, his tenure only lasted one more season.

A year later, after a quarterfinal sweep by the Montreal Canadiens and while the family vacationed three hours north of the city at their cottage in Haliburton, Ontario, where Jim ran a hockey camp and David spent his summers on the ice, the phone call came.

On the other end of the line was NHL executive Harry Sinden, calling to tell Jim about a job opening.

"I already have a job, and I'm going to stay with it," Jim replied.

"You haven't heard?" Sinden answered. "You've been fired."

Ballard had fired him, replacing him with Punch Imlach, his predecessor of a decade earlier. But Ballard hadn't told him. Sinden had—at least, accidentally.

The job opening was apparently the directorship of the NHL Central Scouting Bureau. Four years earlier, as Jim expanded the Leafs' own scouting operation, he had pushed the league to start a centralized scouting service to which every team could have access. Sinden knew when word got out that its first director, Jack Button, was taking a scouting position with the Washington Capitals, an out-of-work Jim might be interested in the gig.

A second call came later from league president John Ziegler, who, with the prompting of former president Clarence Campbell, formally offered Jim the job.

Jim took it and over the course of the next decade led the service into the modern era, adding scouts and building out an international infrastructure that expanded the league's scouting and recruitment efforts globally in a time when top players were still choosing the rival WHA over the NHL.

In time, Jim's status at the league took on an almost mythical quality. In 1986, he was promoted and became the league's executive director of hockey operations on top of his Central Scouting leadership. In 1992, he hired his own replacement, Frank Bonello, as the third director of scouting for the league. By the turn of the century, he was the chairman of the Hockey Hall of Fame's (HHOF) selection committee and the NHL's senior vice president of hockey operations. Under his leadership, the league introduced video goal reviews.

He held his role with the league's hockey operations department into his old age, representing the NHL at all major functions and regularly handing out top awards for decades. In 2007, while tending to his health on hiatus from his chairmanship of the HHOF's selection committee, Jim was elected to the HHOF in the builder category. After a heart attack in 2009 and treatment for amyloidosis, a blood disorder, in 2011, the Canadian Hockey League renamed the player of the game awards for its top prospects in recognition of Jim's contributions to junior hockey. Throughout the 2010s, Jim continued to serve as the master of ceremonies for the NHL draft, attending every draft but one from 1963 in Montreal to 2018 in Dallas. He died in his Toronto home on October 30, 2019, five days before his 84th birthday, after bladder cancer had worked its way into his body's soft tissue, eventually overtaking him. After his passing, the NHL renamed its top honour for managers the Jim Gregory General Manager of the Year Award.

Left to right, the HHOF class of 2007: Ron Francis (player), Al MacInnis (player), Jim Gregory (builder), Mark Messier (player), and Scott Stevens (player). *(AP Photo/Adrian Wyld, The Canadian Press)*

Today, when David remembers his father, he chokes up. David was born in 1961 and named after Father Bauer, on whom Jim relied for advice and friendship until Bauer's passing in 1988. David realizes how spoiled he was as a kid, soaking in hockey history as it happened. Because Jim spent so much time on the road for work, David wishes he'd cherished every moment when he was home more. He laughs about his dad learning of his firing through the grapevine, a story Jim told repeatedly later in his life.

After playing Junior B with the Markham Royals and Port Credit Titans, David played NCAA hockey at Elmira College, then a Division II school, before starting a career in banking. But after trying it in the real world, David knew he wanted to live a hockey life like the one his father had. In the early 1990s, David pounced when one of his clients solicited his help as a consultant for the launch of the American Hockey League's Syracuse Crunch. After David helped the team find its footing, it then asked for his help finding a general manager.

"I asked them, 'Well, what kind of person are you looking for?' and they said, 'Well, someone like a Dave Gregory who has a business background and a hockey background.' I said, 'Well, why don't you ask Dave Gregory?'" David said with a laugh, recalling the way he got his first job in hockey.

After the Crunch, in a time when the AHL and IHL were competing for aspiring NHLers and the AHL was offering favourable deals to prospective owners (including paying for the team over a 10-year period) in an effort to align a club with every NHL team, David worked with a pair of childhood friends to buy an AHL franchise. He went on to lease the Carolina Monarchs and relocate them to New Haven, where he served two seasons as the team's owner, general manager, and president.

Then, in 2002, when David was in Philadelphia doing some part-time NHL scouting and Jim was there to convince Flyers assistant coach E.J. McGuire to consider joining NHL Central Scouting, McGuire and David ended up sitting together at the game that night. Coincidentally, they knew each other independently of Jim. Before David had gone to

Elmira College, McGuire had tried to recruit him to play at State University of New York College with its Brockport Golden Eagles. Then, when David was in Syracuse and New Haven, McGuire was with the Hartford Wolf Pack.

"Well, if I go there, would you come to Central Scouting with me?" McGuire asked David at the Flyers game.

"Well, sure, let's talk about it," David said.

Though he questioned whether he should take the job, worrying about concerns of nepotism through the obvious ties to his father, David eventually joined NHL Central Scouting the same year McGuire did in 2005.

To this day, David still works at NHL Central Scouting in his father's absence, managing its group of scouts under current director Dan Marr. And when he scouts the sport's best young players, he reminds himself constantly of the advice his dad used to give him when he was a player, informing his evaluations with Jim's tips.

"I learned a lot about what he thought about players when he evaluated my game," David said. "A lot of people could pick out Sidney Crosby as the best player in a junior game. But it's how do you pick out the other guys, the guys that could be that other player that you get later on in the draft? So learning as a young player myself what I had to improve on to be a better player really taught me about what to look for in other players."

Because Jim stressed the importance of a 200-foot game or gave due credit to the complementary defencemen who could play alongside someone with the talent of a Salming, David learned to appreciate those subtle skills, and the nuances of the game, through him.

Later in life, when Jim's health began to deteriorate and David would come through Toronto on one of his scouting trips, they got to scout local games together. David calls those moments some of the best of his life. And he never stopped learning new things from his dad. Right until the end, Jim could spot the best players on the ice below them, even as he stepped away from the day-to-day of his various titles with the NHL.

"It wasn't his job to know, 'Hey, there are 12 players in this game, some that are barely going to make the list and some that are going to be at the top of the list,' but he very quickly could know who those players were or would ask, 'Who's that player?'" David said. "It was really fun to see how quickly he understood what a talented and complete hockey player was."

Jim's hockey life has been passed on to a third Gregory generation now, too. David has three sons of his own and his middle son, Lyle, worked in the Blackhawks' hockey operations department, developing a player evaluation tool that blends in-person scouting analysis with analytics. After leaving the Blackhawks, Lyle started Champ DAT with that software. David's youngest son, Kade, also started his own company, Hockey DNA, to help young players choose the right path for their hockey development, whether that's finding the college that makes the most sense for them or the camp that does.

"There's this evaluator-teacher thing in all of us. It comes from what all started with my dad," David said.

David describes his father as tough and resilient, but also as an innovator who was "so darn humble all the time," the kind of person who would credit countless other names for his success before mentioning his own or would tell anyone who would listen that he was just carrying on what he'd learned from others.

One of Jim's favourite stories to tell was one David's Grade 7 teacher had told him during a parent-teacher interview. The morning before the interview, David's teacher had gone around the room asking each of the students what their parents did. David famously answered plainly, "No, my dad doesn't work, he's in hockey."

Now 61, David has learned to view life in his father's shadow the same way.

"There has never been anyone like him when you look at what his roots were, where he came from, and what he accomplished. But he always just loved what he did and could not get enough of it," David said. "I've got some of that gene in me too, because it's not real work. I always use that line with people. People ask me what it's like working in hockey and I always say, 'It's better than a real job.'"

Even in Jim's moment in the limelight, when he was inducted alongside a legendary HHOF class that also included Mark Messier, Al McInnis, Ron Francis, and Scott Stevens, he spent his speech explaining his genuine disbelief and naming other names.

Al MacNeil. Colin Campbell. Mike Murphy. Gary Bettman. Bill Daly. Father David Bauer. Stafford Smythe. His son, David; daughters, Andrea, Maureen, and Valeri; and wife, Rosalie. They were the Hall of Famers, he insisted during his acceptance speech, tears streaming down his face. It was their homage, he said.

"It's overwhelming. I tell my friends this: I don't think I deserve to be in the Hall of Fame," Jim said, looking over a crowd of the people he'd helped shape, including Sittler and Salming, who both made sure they were in the audience for his induction.

He talked of the four other inductees and how he'd still be general manager of the Leafs if they were on his team. He talked about being in hockey as a privilege and all the many places around the world it had taken him. He argued his induction belonged to minor hockey parents, officials, coaches, and volunteers.

"It's each one of you people who do that who are the true builders of the game, who work tirelessly with little fanfare behind the scenes to provide little kids with the opportunity to play the game that all of us love so much," he said.

As he finished his speech, his hands shook. He licked his index finger, and he flipped the pages in front of him on the podium.

"How often does someone get a chance to live a dream?" he asked.

He paused, trying to choke out his last three words.

"I did," he said, raising a fist. "Thanks."

David will never forget that moment. But that was his dad. Earnest, true to himself, and filled to the brim with humility.

"He didn't think that he was in the class of what he actually was in a lot of ways. And those guys were just like, 'Jim's the real stud here.' It's amazing the things those players said to me and my family," David remembered. "It was just an unreal experience."

In the years since Jim's 2007 induction into the Hall of Fame, David has received similar messages to the ones Messier, Francis, Stevens, and McInnis gave him about his dad, in rinks across the hockey world in his own role with NHL Central Scouting.

He gets them every day. Every. Single. Day.

Your dad was so helpful for me.

Your dad is one of the greatest people.

I can't thank your dad enough.

You can't believe how much your dad helped me.

All that love and admiration, a love and admiration that is universally shared in the hockey world, came to a head for Jim at his last draft in 2018, too.

The entire Gregory family didn't know it would be his last until he told those who were in Dallas (David with NHL Central Scouting, Lyle with the Blackhawks, and Kade as a volunteer) a few days before it started.

When deputy commissioner Bill Daly stepped to the podium on the Saturday morning of the second day to tell the hockey world that it would be Jim's last draft, he received a standing ovation that prevailed through their speeches.

"Jim is an institution at our league and on this weekend," Daly said amid applause. "But today will be the last time that he calls out the names of young men selected in an NHL draft."

Daly paused, allowing the man to his right the time to take it in. Then he finished.

"On a personal note, I can honestly say that Jim is one of the finest human beings I know, and I have been truly privileged and honoured both to work with him and to call him a friend. Please join me in thanking the incomparable Jim Gregory for decades of tireless service to our game," Daly said, extending his hands to Gregory, who had his own clenched behind his back, as if embarrassed.

"How am I going to talk now?" Gregory said after finally stepping to the empty podium and lowering the mic to his mouth. "Thank you everyone very much. It's my honour to participate in this draft, in this wonderful city of Dallas. We'll start off the second round. The first pick in the second round belongs to the Buffalo Sabres."

In the hours that followed, as each team made its selections, the league's general managers and chief scouts grabbed microphones of their own to thank Jim for everything he'd given to the game in advance of their selections.

He was their guy. The draft guy. And they wanted him to know it.

"He had been a part of just about every guy in that room's life in one way or another. It was everyone else getting to hear what I hear every time I'm at the rink," David said. "It was very emotional for my dad. I grew up with a dad who taught me toughness in a lot of ways, but he was also such a loving guy and as I got older I realized how emotional he is. I was just so happy to hear what people said about him, that's for sure."

In the final year of Jim's life, when his cancer developed and his condition grew graver, Campbell, Daly, Bettman, and Marr encouraged David to move home to Toronto so that he could be around his dad as much as possible in his final days.

He was the same guy right until the end, according to David. For a while, people from around the hockey world came by to visit and share stories with Jim almost daily. Bettman. Daly. Campbell. Sittler. McDonald. Bobby Orr. They all rotated through, sitting in the Gregory family living room to chat and reminisce.

"It got to the point where my mom said, 'We've really got to stop the visits,' because of where we knew things were headed. But when he had the strength to, he would want those visits. And that's when he would perk up the most. He would be back to his old self, and it would be crazy. For a few minutes, he would be telling stories and having people laugh," David said. "And he made everyone else the star all the time. He was always talking about how he was amongst royalty when anyone came to visit him. They were the ones that were the special ones."

2

THE FIRST PICK

THE INAUGURAL NHL Amateur Draft was held at the Queen Elizabeth Hotel in Montreal on June 5, 1963. It was created by NHL president Clarence Campbell to eliminate the sponsorship system and level the playing field for recruitment. Only 16-year-olds (players who turned 17 between August 1, 1963 and July 31, 1964) were eligible.

From 1963 until 1967, when sponsored teams were officially eliminated, sponsored players could not be picked, and the Leafs got to retain the rights to the top prospects on their farm teams. There were just four rounds and 24 picks in the first amateur draft, though teams were given the option to defer selections and just 21 players were selected in total in 1963. To determine the draft order, the league's six teams got to choose their slot according to how low they finished in the 1962–63 standings. But the standings would not establish the order every year. Instead, teams would move up one slot in each consecutive draft. That meant that if the last-place team wanted to pick first overall in the 1963 draft, it would slide to the bottom of the first round and pick sixth in 1964. The Bruins, who'd just finished at the bottom in 1962–63, elected to pick third, guaranteeing a top-three pick at each of the first three drafts. The Leafs, who'd just won the 1963 Stanley Cup in five games over the Red Wings, were given whichever slot remained after the other five teams had chosen theirs. Predictably, they got the last pick of each round.

Walt McKechnie, the team's sixth overall selection, was living in an apartment building at 1011 Adelaide Street North in London, Ontario, when the call came.

"Walt McKechnie?" said the unfamiliar voice of Bob Davidson, the Leafs' chief scout, at the other end of the line.

"Yeah?" Walt replied.

"I just wanted to let you know that the Toronto Maple Leafs have made you our first-round draft choice. We would like to meet with you to go over the details."

"Well, sure, I guess, tell me when."

"Can I talk to your parents?"

"Well, it's only my mother," Walt said, passing off the phone.

Until that moment, Walt had no idea what the draft was and no clue that the Leafs had ever even watched him play.

He was raised by his single mother, Kay; his grandmother, Edith; and his aunt, Helen, after his parents separated when he was four years old. He fell in love with hockey while sitting on the floor in the apartment with a cup of tea and toast with peanut butter, staying up until the second intermission to watch the Leafs on the family's black-and-white TV before bed. He fell in love with playing the sport on the pond across from the apartment complex, which he and other kids from the building would chop a hole in, scrape, and flood themselves. In the early 1950s, when Walt began playing organized Peewee hockey, there were four rinks in London (North, South, East, and West), one house league team per rink and age group, and travelling teams that picked the best players from all four rinks for games against nearby towns like Lucan and St. Mary's. Walt practically lived at the North Rink, an open-air arena a few blocks from his apartment. As a young boy, he drove his mother crazy sneaking out at night to play.

"You're not going out tonight," Kay would tell him.

And each night he would smirk when she went down to do laundry, grab his stick and skates, and tell Edith or his sister, Kathy, that they knew where to find him as he left to a familiar warning.

"You're going to get in trouble," Edith or Kathy would tell him.

A couple hours later, Kay would show up at the rink to shout at him and the other kids, all much older, who still lingered on the ice.

In time, Walt became the North Rink's ringer. Each week, the house league games were scheduled so that the Peewees (ages 11 and 12) played first, the Bantams (ages 13 and 14) played second, and the Midgets (ages 15 and 16) played last, and the coach for the Bantam team would walk down the hall after the Peewees played to throw a jersey over Walt's shoulders so that he could play again, followed an hour later by the Midget coach with the same idea. At 12, Walt was playing on five teams: the North's house league teams for all three age groups and London's Peewee and Bantam travel teams.

Kay, who worked a full-time job at local printing company Wright Lithographing and couldn't afford to own a car, didn't have the time or the means to attend many of Walt's games.

Instead, Jack Webb, who owned Webb's Variety nearby the McKechnie apartment and whose sons Mike and Tom played hockey with Walt on those older North teams, became his father figure, offering to load his gear into his Chevrolet station wagon and drive him to games.

Kay also couldn't afford to buy her son new skates, so he wore used skates that were several sizes too big for him as he grew into them for most of his childhood. It wasn't until he was 12 and spending all his nights and weekends at the rink playing on those five teams that he got his first new pair of skates on a visit to see Helen at her job at London's Eaton's department store.

After arriving at the store, Helen, who worked in the fur department, told Walt to go down to the sporting department. There, Walt was greeted by a surprise she'd lined up.

"You're Walt McKechnie, Helen's nephew, aren't you?" said a stranger as he stepped into the sporting goods area.

"Yes?" Walt answered, confused.

"Sit down, son."

"Why?"

"I'm going to fit you with brand-new Tackaberry skates," the man said, hinting at an arrangement Helen had made to pay for them and fitting him with a pair of what are today known as CCM Tacks.

A few minutes later, the skates were his and the man handed him a jar of Dubbin (a wax product for leather that was commonly used to soften and waterproof skates) and told him he better take good care of them.

As he became a teenager, those skates lived under his bed and Helen promised to replace them whenever they wore down so long as he promised to behave.

Walt didn't always live up to his end of the bargain. He was mouthy and full of attitude, two things that today he thinks link back to his father's absence in his life and the strong sense of independence he had from a very young age. He was quicker to rebel than to obey authority and didn't take much in his life seriously.

It wasn't until he was 14 that his attitude began to change. He was still technically supposed to be a Bantam-aged player, but he'd seen an ad in the newspaper calling on "all local homebrews" to try out for the London Nationals, the local Junior B team. Walt decided on a whim to audition for the team. When the tryouts were over and he was on his way out of the rink, Art Lawson, the team's general manager, pulled him aside and told him that he'd set up a meeting with his mother to discuss the potential of him playing on the team.

That night, Lawson showed up at their apartment door and joined them at their kitchen table.

"Well, Mrs. McKechnie, we'd like your son to play Junior B hockey for us," Lawson said. "But there's one problem."

"What's the problem?" Kay asked.

"Well, he's going to be playing against guys that are 18, 19, and 20 years old, and he could get hurt," Lawson answered.

"Well, what do you think?" Kay said, turning to her son.

"I want to play, Mom," Walt answered.

The following season, while playing for the Nationals as a 15-year-old in advance of a draft day that he didn't even know was possible, Walt got his act together at the rink and began to take hockey more seriously. He struggled to humble himself away from the rink, though.

At Beal Tech, his high school, he had trouble concentrating and rarely handed in assignments. Though he was never violent, the school eventually expelled him for bad behaviour and poor grades. On his way out of the school and down the steps with Kay, she cried and screamed at him with a different tone than she ever had before.

"Mom, don't worry about a thing; I'm going to make it to the NHL someday," he told her.

"There's six teams! Do you know how many players there are!?" she yelled back between breaths.

So when he picked up that phone call from the Leafs a few months later, passing off Davidson to his mom so that they could make arrangements to meet and go over what it meant, Walt was a high school dropout and hockey was his only path forward.

Within a week, Davidson made the two-hour trip from Toronto to London to meet with Kay and Walt. There, back in that apartment at their kitchen table, Davidson told Walt that he would have to stop playing football and baseball (he was a pitcher in the local Eager Beaver Baseball Association and a quarterback on the high school football team before he was expelled).

After Walt signed over his rights to the Maple Leafs, Davidson gave Kay $100 and told them they'd be in touch once he was 18 if they were interested in inviting him to camp.

The following season, when the Leafs were without a second sponsored team after they amalgamated the Neil McNeil Maroons into the Marlboros, they decided to sponsor the Nationals, hoping their involvement with the team could facilitate a move to the newly constructed London Gardens and a promotion into the OHA to play at the Junior A level. Though the OHA refused at first, the Leafs sponsored the Nationals to two Junior B titles in 1964 and 1965. When the Nationals were finally admitted into the Junior A level for the 1965–66 OHA season, Walt stayed to play Junior A while the Junior B team moved to nearby Ingersoll. In Walt's second year in the OHA and fifth year on the Nationals, the Leafs then sent legendary goalie Turk Broda to London to serve as the farm team's head coach.

Broda became Walt's mentor, the first hockey coach to understand what made him tick and push him and his top teammates Jim Dorey (a fourth-round pick of the Leafs in 1964) and Garry Unger. In a time when the role of a coach was to motivate and there was little to no attention paid to systems or tactics, Broda was the ultimate motivator. In Walt, Broda recognized that the only way he was going to be able to rein in his top player's outspoken nature was to be harder on him than everyone else.

One night in Montreal in a game between the Nationals and the Jr. Canadiens at the Montreal Forum, Walt came to the bench sulking after a handful of bad shifts to start the game, and Broda wouldn't let him off the ice.

"You get back out there you big, lazy son of a bitch!" Broda yelled at him when he arrived at the door, leaving him on for the final 10 minutes of the period.

Walt took to that approach, never complaining again. And when the season was over, his game had reached a new level under Broda's guidance, with 59 points in 48 games as the team's second-leading scorer to Unger as a 19-year-old.

The following season, after the Leafs won the 1967 Stanley Cup, Walt, Unger, and Dorey were each invited to their 1967–68 training camp in Peterborough, Ontario. Walt attended thinking he still had a year of junior left and found himself in awe when he walked into a dressing room full of his idols, joining a group that included Tim Horton, George Armstrong, Bob Pulford, Ron Ellis, Dave Keon, Frank Mahovlich, and Johnny Bower.

Though Walt woke up each morning expecting to be sent home by the Leafs, they called him in at the end of the camp intent on signing him. Walt spent most of the meeting in shock, stumbling over his words until they eventually gave him an offer, presenting him with a C form, the most restrictive of three standard agreements young players could sign at the time. (A forms required the player attend a tryout, B forms allowed teams to sign a player for a bonus, and C forms could only be signed at 18 and tied a player's rights to their team.) The offer stipulated that the Leafs would pay him $3,000 to sign, $5,000 to play in the minors, and $10,000 to play in the NHL. All C forms also stipulated that while the team was only making a one-year commitment to the player, the terms of the contract were binding in perpetuity. So players were required to show up to training camp and play wherever they were assigned under the agreement, but there was no free market for their services and the team could trade the player or re-sign him at the previously agreed upon cash payment for each new season.

After asking for some time to think about it, Walt convened with Bower, Pulford, and Armstrong at Peterborough's Empress Hotel, where the team was staying, to ask their advice. Armstrong was the first to speak up when Walt was done explaining the offer, insisting the Leafs were trying to swindle him out of a few thousand dollars because he was a London kid and he didn't come up as a Marlboro.

"Kid, you're going to play in this league. You're a good player, you've had a good camp, and they're screwing you for money. Don't sign for that money," Armstrong said. "They're paying the Marlies guys $5,000 to sign, $7,000 to play in the minors, and $12,000 to play in the NHL, and you're every bit as good as them."

When Pulford and Bower agreed, Walt set out to ask for what the Marlboros were apparently getting. The next day, when he gave the Leafs his demands, general manager Punch Imlach's response was swift.

"No," Imlach said.

"OK, then what are my choices?" Walt asked

"Go home and play junior," Imlach answered plainly.

Unwilling to back down, Walt told Imlach he'd do just that, packed his bags, called Broda to tell him he was coming back to London, and left Peterborough on the first bus south to Kitchener.

After driving up from London to pick up Walt in Kitchener, Broda spent the car ride back admonishing him for rejecting the offer.

"I can't teach you anything. You've got to play pro hockey; you've got to play against men if you're going to become a hockey player. Down here you're going to get frustrated," Broda warned.

After a couple of weeks of practicing and one game with the Nationals, which was exactly as frustrating as Broda told him it would be, Lawson then followed up with Walt to deliver the same message.

"You've got to turn pro," Lawson told him. "I could call Bob Davidson and the Leafs and they could be down here tomorrow and you could sign that form."

Reluctantly, Walt eventually caved, asking Broda and Lawson to set up a meeting.

A few days later they all gathered—Walt, Kay, Broda, Lawson, and Davidson—at a nearby Holiday Inn. When it was over, Walt, still bitter about the offer, threw his pen down on the table.

"I'll show you you're wrong. I'm going to show you that I can play in the NHL," he told Davidson with his usual bravado.

He stood up and turned to Kay.

"Let's go," he said as they left for the bus stop.

Unimpressed by Walt's attitude, Davidson and the Leafs called the next morning to deliver a message of their own, telling him he had to report to the Phoenix Roadrunners in the WHL, then a top minor professional league. A Phoenix-based ownership group had purchased the Leafs' professional farm team, the Victoria Maple Leafs, and as part of their plans to relocate the team from British Columbia to Arizona, they were travelling down the West Coast of the United States playing exhibition games. Davidson told Walt that he had to get to Toronto to catch a flight to Seattle to meet the team.

"Well, fuck," Walt said, pulling the phone away from his ear. "Mom, did you hear that?"

Early on with the Roadrunners, Walt was extremely unhappy. The team's coach, Alf Pike, was nothing like Broda and offered virtually no guidance to the team, leaving the players to run it themselves. The older players were tough on Walt, constantly yelling at him to move the puck. Walt, who had better hands than his peers after growing up on the pond, wasn't used to that style, preferring to hang onto the puck. One day, after the players had been particularly hard on him, Walt debated quitting and called Webb for advice.

"These guys are picking on me," Walt complained. "They're always yelling at me and treating me like shit."

"You shut up and listen," Webb quickly answered. "They're trying to help you. When they quit talking to you, then you're in trouble. They can see that you've got talent and they're trying to show you how to play a pro game."

Once he realized that was their approach, Walt became a sponge, and his outgoing personality came back out. Bob Kabel, his linemate, took a special interest in him.

"Hey, kid, just give me the puck for a second. I'll give it back to you. Don't worry, I know you want it. It's your puck," Kabel would joke with him.

Tom Polanic, the team's goon, became Walt's protector, knowing that Walt was a better talker than fighter.

A couple of months into his first season with the Roadrunners, Walt had become one of the team's best players when Pike pulled him aside to let him know that he had to call Wren Blair, the head coach and general manager of the Minnesota North Stars, one of six new NHL expansion teams during the 1967–68 season, because they'd given the Maple Leafs three minor league players for his rights. Because Walt didn't have an agent until much later in his career, he called Blair himself.

"Yeah, Walt, you're now a member of the Minnesota North Stars and we're going to bring you up here soon to play a game and introduce you to the new players, but you'll probably finish the year in Phoenix," Blair told him, before he'd ever played a game for the Leafs.

Walt won the WHL's rookie of the year award that season, finishing with 54 points in 67 games. Like Blair promised, he was then promoted to the North Stars, making his NHL debut late in their regular season and playing in the entirety of their nine-game playoff run. In the semifinals, after the North Stars had upset the higher-seeded Los Angeles Kings in the first round, Walt scored with 3:11 left in Game 7 against the St. Louis Blues to give Minnesota a 1–0 lead, putting them on the brink of the Stanley Cup Final until Dickie Moore scored 31 seconds later and the Blues won in double overtime.

In the years that followed, after bouncing between pro levels with the North Stars, Walt established himself as valuable centreman in the league. But he never really stayed put in one place, in large part due to his attitude. After the North Stars, he played three seasons as a top player with the California Golden Seals. Then he was traded to the Boston Bruins by way of the New York Rangers and the intra-league draft process, playing less than a full season there under head coach Don Cherry before he was dealt to the Detroit Red

Wings. In Detroit, he became a star, putting together back-to-back 25-goal seasons and leading the team in scoring with 82 points in 1975–76. In April 1977, he represented Canada at the Ice Hockey World Championships in Vienna, Austria, scoring seven points in 10 games en route to a bronze medal loss to the Soviet Union on a team that featured Hall of Famers like Ellis, who he'd met all those years earlier at Leafs camp, and Phil and Tony Esposito.

Though he didn't make his NHL debut with the Leafs, Walt eventually found his way back to the team that made him its first ever draft choice.

The series of events that led to his return to Toronto started in the off-season after the 1977 World Championships, when he was dealt from the Red Wings to the Washington Capitals. In Washington, Walt got off on the wrong foot with head coach Tom McVie, who he thought was incompetent and frequently expressed as much. The Capitals, then in their fourth season, were dreadful, at one point going 20 games without a win. McVie blamed Walt for his disrespectful attitude and the toxic culture that had developed through him and close friends and teammates Gary "Axe" Smith and Garnet "Ace" Bailey, who'd helped him speak up. Twenty-six games into the season, after starting with a 3–18–5 record, McVie had Walt traded to the Cleveland Barons, a team in an even worse spot and in the midst of its second and final season in the league.

In Cleveland, there were many nights when the Barons hardly had enough players to dress a lineup. At the end of the season, the team's owners, George and Gord Gunn, managed to merge the Barons with the North Stars and the two rosters were combined. The following year, after showing up to North Stars camp to compete for one roster with two rosters' worth of players, Walt found himself playing under a familiar face in head coach and general manager Lou Nanne, who'd broken into the NHL as a player with the North Stars a decade earlier in 1967–68, the same year Walt had.

Realizing that the North Stars had depth down the middle and knowing that friends Don Maloney, Darryl Sittler, Dave Hutchinson, and Pat Boutette were in Leafs general manager Jim Gregory's ear about trading for him as a second or third line centre, Walt approached Nanne in training camp to ask if he would do him a favour and send him home. Though Nanne said he wouldn't guarantee a trade, he vowed to look into it and eventually worked out a deal with the Leafs just a couple of days before the start of the 1978–79 season.

After getting the call while staying at a hotel in Bloomington, Minnesota, where the North Stars played, Walt got on a flight to Buffalo and played in the Leafs' last exhibition game the following night, surrounded by some of his best friends in the sport.

In Toronto, a 31-year-old Walt arrived as the team's second-oldest player, fitting in perfectly under Gregory and head coach Roger Neilson, with whom he clicked instantly. He finished fifth on the team in scoring, rejuvenating his career with a third 25-goal season and 61 points in 79 games. Every time he bumped into Gregory around the rink, he thanked him for making him a Leaf. That 1978–79 Leafs team had better chemistry than any he'd ever been a part of. Even Harold Ballard, the team's notoriously hard-nosed owner, developed a good bond with the team and was nothing but friendly to Walt, often sitting next to him on team flights, joining the players in the sauna after games, or circling through the dressing room to stir the pot and poke fun at the team's toughest player, Tiger Williams, while the players were getting dressed.

"You know boys, we'd have a pretty good hockey team if we had some toughness on the left side," Ballard once said to Williams, prompting a wrestling match between the owner and his player on the dressing room floor.

Though the Leafs got swept by the titanic Canadiens (who went on to win their fourth consecutive Stanley Cup) in the first round of the playoffs, they lost the final two games of the series in overtime and Canadiens star Larry Robinson told each of them in the handshake line that he thought they were the second-best team in the league.

When the season was over, though, Ballard fired Gregory and Neilson, hiring Floyd Smith as head coach and his long-time friend Punch Imlach as the new general manager. Under Imlach, everything changed and the talented Leafs team that had shown so much promise a year earlier was dismantled. By the time Walt showed up to training camp for his second season with the Leafs, the roster looked significantly different. Imlach had removed the team's ping pong table and juice fridge from the dressing room, instituted a suit-and-tie dress code, and banned beer from team flights and bus rides after the game. Imlach and Sittler, then the team's captain, quickly butted heads over Imlach's public criticisms of players and, later, Imlach's decision to place Sittler's best friend Lanny McDonald on waivers, eventually trading him to the Colorado Rockies in a move all the players agreed was meant to undermine Sittler's role on the team—and one that prompted Sittler to rip the captain's C off of his jersey.

In time, Walt, as he always had before, began to speak up about the way the team was being mismanaged. Things came to a head at a practice in early February that season. After surrendering a combined 24 goals in four consecutive losses to open the month, Smith decided the players were going to run 3-on-0 rushes for the entire hour. Forty-five minutes into it, knowing that goalies Paul Harrison and Mike Palmateer were exhausted, Walt skated by his coach and challenged his approach.

"This is really interesting," he said sarcastically.

"Why's that?" Smith barked back at him.

"I've been in this league for over a decade, and I haven't experienced a 3-on-0," Walt answered.

"Oh, so you know everything, huh?" Smith asked again.

"I know one thing: we couldn't get the puck out of our own end if we picked it up and threw it into the stands or tried to carry it out with a basket," Walt said. Smith turned to face him mid-sentence and yelled, "Get off the ice, you asshole! Get off the ice!"

A few minutes later, while Walt got undressed in the room and Smith punished the players by skating them for the remainder of the practice, he heard a stick smashing against a garbage can. Maloney sauntered into the dressing room.

"What's going on now, Dan?" Walt asked his friend.

"I told Floyd you were right and that we should be practicing coming out of our own zone and he kicked me off the ice," Maloney said.

A couple of days later, when the Leafs left for a six-game road trip through New York, Chicago, Winnipeg, St. Louis, and Colorado, the team left Walt in Toronto without communicating to him what to do. He spent the next two weeks skating with the Marlies, who were nice enough to allow him to practice after his agent at the time, Bill Watters, had asked. He knew, though, that his days were numbered. When the team returned from the road trip, Smith pulled him aside at practice in advance of a back-to-back against the Flyers and the Red Wings to tell him that he was going to play but that he would only play on the penalty kill and power play. After picking up assists in both games and being named third star in one of them, Walt thought he might get to stick around. The day after the back-to-back, March 3, 1980, Walt spent the afternoon of the team's day off at a pub the players frequented in nearby Oakville when Maloney, who lived in the area, showed up with some news.

"Where the hell have you been all day? You've been traded to Colorado," Maloney told him.

The next morning, Watters told Walt, who was a little hungover, to go to Maple Leaf Gardens to collect his gear and fly to Colorado, ending his two-season run with his childhood team. Walt finished that season with the Rockies and played three more in the NHL. He finished his career on a second stint with the Red Wings, registering 43 points in 64 games at the age of 35 in 1982–83. Though he'd finished fourth on the team in scoring and he wanted desperately to play one last season so that he could reach 1,000 NHL games, Watters couldn't find Walt an NHL contract that summer and he played his final year of professional hockey with the minor pro Central Hockey League's Salt Lake Golden Eagles before retiring at the age of 37.

Today, Walt has a home on Eagle Lake in Haliburton, Ontario, three hours north of Toronto. He was introduced to the area by Blair at the end of that very first playoff run with the North Stars in 1968, when his coach offered to put up him and his wife Suzanne in a cottage if he would spend his summer teaching at the Haliburton Hockey Haven, a camp started by Blair and Gregory that has famously welcomed Bobby Orr, Johnny Bower, Red Kelly and others as instructors over the years. Walt raised his four daughters, Katie, Shannon, Hunter, and Tatum in the area. In 1986, he opened McKeck's, a family restaurant on Highland Street in Haliburton's downtown. He owned and operated the restaurant for nearly two and a half decades, expanding it from 65 seats to 245 seats before selling it in 2009. He is now serving his third term on Haliburton's town council, a position he has held since 2010. McKeck's persists, a staple of the town.

Now in his seventies, Walt credits his mother as his biggest fan and realizes how she and his sister stuck with him even though he was an "asshole." He remembers thinking, *He must care about me* when Broda left him out there for that final 10 minutes at the Forum. He remembers the unbelievable—and confused—feeling he had when Davidson told him *the* Leafs had selected him sixth overall. He still can't believe the things McVie did in Washington. He recognizes the role his mouthiness played in his winding career path but still doesn't shy away from speaking his mind in his role as a councillor for Haliburton's Ward 5. He glows about that first season under Neilson, a coach he says taught him as much as any other. He laughs about how the Leafs have traded him twice but to this day have never told him so. He still can't believe Ballard "lost his mind and hired Punch back," insisting the game had passed Punch by and describing his tactics as "barbaric." He remembers fondly living in downtown Toronto and bumming rides to and from the rink in the back of the van used by the team's trainers.

Only five of the 21 players selected in the inaugural 1963 draft went on to play in NHL games. The Leafs did well, drafting three of those players. Walt accumulated 606 points in 955 career NHL games, finishing second in the draft class in scoring to Pete Mahovolich, taken second overall by the Red Wings.

Though Walt didn't play for the Leafs until later in his career, he'll never forget those two seasons.

"It was the highlight of my career. Being a Leaf? Are you kidding?" he said. "Once you're a Leaf, you're always a Leaf. It's not the same with other teams. Never does a day go by where someone doesn't notice, even if you were just a journeyman like me."

3

BRUCE BOUDREAU, RANDY CARLYLE, AND A 1970S HISTORY OF COACHES

A **FTER THE LEAFS'** four Stanley Cups of the 1960s, the 1970s were marked by two things. The first was the league's rapid expansion. After doubling in size from six to 12 teams in 1967, the league expanded a further four times in the 1970s, ballooning to 14 teams in 1970 with the arrival of the Buffalo Sabres and Vancouver Canucks, 16 teams in 1972 with the introduction of New York's second team (the Islanders) and the Atlanta Flames, 18 teams in 1974 with the Washington Capitals and the short-lived Kansas City Scouts, and then 21 teams in 1979 with the addition of the Edmonton Oilers, Hartford Whalers, Quebec Nordiques, and Winnipeg

Jets, losing one team (the Cleveland Barons) along the way. The last of those expansions also coincided with the second defining feature of the '70s—the emergence of the World Hockey Association (WHA) as a legitimate adversary to the NHL. The WHA launched in 1971 and began play the following year, disrupting the hockey landscape by luring dozens of the NHL's players, including two-time league MVP and three-time scoring champ Bobby Hull and later names like Gordie Howe, Frank Mahovolich, and Paul Henderson. The WHA also shook things up with the NHL Amateur Draft when its teams took scouting beyond North America's borders and turned it into a global enterprise with the recruitment of European stars like Ulf Nilsson, Anders Hedberg, and Vaclav Nedomansky, all while attracting many of the game's brightest North American–bred players, including Wayne Gretzky, Mike Gartner, Mark Howe, and Mark Messier.

The Leafs, as they had begun to post-expansion in the late '60s, lagged behind on all fronts, failing to make it out of the first round of the playoffs—when they didn't miss them altogether—in the first five postseasons of the new decade. At the draft tables of the '70s, even after sponsored clubs went extinct, the Leafs continued to turn to Canadian pipelines for the bulk of their draft choices. The results of that approach were mixed, but the staying power of the Leafs brand helped them win their competitions with the WHA on some key picks, including future Hall of Famers Darryl Sittler (taken eighth overall in 1970) and Lanny McDonald (taken fourth overall in 1973), as well as fan favourites Ian Turnbull (taken 15th in 1973) and Dave "Tiger" Williams (taken 31st in 1974).

The Leafs' draft results in the second half of the decade were much bleaker, however, and paved the way for the team's undoing into the early 1980s. From 1975 to '79, just one player picked by the Leafs, John Anderson (drafted 11th overall in 1977), was retained for multiple seasons by the team.

There *was* something unmistakable about the Leafs drafts of the late '70s, though, and that's their numerous selections of future NHL coaches and managers, people who are today known more for their careers on benches and in front offices than as players for the Leafs

They are Bruce Boudreau, Ron Wilson, Ken Holland, Randy Carlyle, Joel Quenneville, and Anderson, and their NHL stories started in Toronto—or with a phone call from its team.

BRUCE BOUDREAU WAS in the basement of his parents' family home in Toronto's Downsview neighbourhood, where Keele Street meets Highway 401 at the city's northern limits, waiting for the call to come with his dad, Norm. The 1975 NHL Amateur Draft was in its usual city—Montreal—but an unusual location—the league's offices—as the NHL tried to keep its picks secret from the WHA.

Boudreau thanks God that he wasn't in attendance because he says he "would have had a conniption" after the way his draft day unfolded. A year before his NHL draft day, he was taken 14th overall by the Minnesota Fighting Saints in the 1974 WHA Draft. The following season, in 1974–75, his NHL draft year, Boudreau was the 19-year-old star of his hometown Marlboros, who still had strong ties with the Leafs even after their sponsorship with the NHL club dissolved—and who were coached by Leafs legend George Armstrong. In 69 games with the team, he won the Ontario Major Junior Hockey League's (the newly formed Tier I major junior level of the OHA) Eddie Powers Trophy as its leading scorer with 68 goals and 165 points, a full 30 more than his nearest teammate.

Two weeks before the June 3 draft was set to take place, Boudreau was celebrating winning the Memorial Cup with those Marlboros when he was approached by then Leafs assistant general manager John McLellan (who'd stepped down from his position as head coach two years earlier to join the management team). McLellan told Boudreau that the Leafs were going to use their sixth overall pick on him, but that they weren't sure if he would still be available. A couple of weeks before that, Boudreau had another meeting with his agent, Alan Eagleson (then a giant in the hockey world and the first director of the NHLPA, later removed from the Order of Canada and Hockey Hall of Fame after he was convicted of defrauding his clients), and agent Bill Watters. The pair had told him that the California Golden Seals, who picked third, had him No. 1 on their list.

So when the draft started and Boudreau was sitting in his basement for "what seemed like forever," he was devastated. And when the call finally came from Eagleson's secretary informing Boudreau that he'd been selected 42nd overall in the third round by the Leafs, his childhood team, he was more upset than happy.

"I wasn't drinking or nothing when McLellan and Eagleson told me those things, so I was ecstatic heading in and that's why the disappointment was in me," Boudreau said. "I didn't know what happened between those times and the draft when I was taken 42nd. That didn't make any sense to me."

His devastation then turned into despondence when he found out that the Leafs had used both of their earlier picks to draft two other centres, Don Ashby and Doug Jarvis.

"Now, so many years later, just being drafted is great. But at the time I was thinking that I would have gone *a lot* higher than I did. When you're young, you can't handle it very well," Boudreau said. "You're expecting so many things and it didn't work out."

The following season, Boudreau had a number of opportunities to join the Leafs, but he was persuaded at each turn to go in a different direction. The first came before the season began when the Leafs and the Fighting Saints offered him identical money, right down to the signing bonuses.

"The Leafs have a lot of centremen right now; why don't you go to the WHA, play the contract, and then we'll sign with the Leafs after that," Eagleson told Boudreau.

Under the advice of Eagleson, Boudreau committed to play in Minnesota. After getting into 30 games with the Fighting Saints, the team then folded midseason and Boudreau had a second opportunity in February to sign with the Leafs and join their farm team in Oklahoma City or sign with the WHA's Indianapolis Racers, who'd taken him first overall in the dispersal draft out of Minnesota. Once more, though, Eagleson, who had a strained-at-the-best-of-times relationship with Toronto's Harold Ballard, pushed Boudreau in another direction.

"I know they're making that movie in Johnstown; go down and make the movie, relax, take this year off, and we'll start fresh next year," Eagleson said.

The movie was *Slap Shot*, and the team was the NAHL's Johnstown Jets. Boudreau did both, playing an on-ice extra in the film while starring for the local team, scoring 60 points in 34 games.

Today, when he looks back on both of those decisions, he just shakes his head.

"It was totally against anything I've ever done. Relax? Are you kidding me? In hindsight, I cannot believe I accepted that, even though making the movie *Slap Shot*, or being a part of it, 44 years later it's so iconic and I still get asked everywhere I go about it," Boudreau said. "Why I didn't go to Toronto or Indianapolis is beyond me, though. I don't get it. I just don't get why that happened."

After feeling like he'd mostly wasted his first year of professional hockey, Boudreau never quite caught back up with his status as a top prospect again. The following season, he signed with the Leafs. Before long, he dropped Eagleson as his agent, an experience that made him represent himself for the next two decades of his career.

"I just didn't believe in agents after that," Boudreau said. "These are things that you look back on as, *Did you make a mistake? Did you do the right thing?* And you listen to your agent at the time. I didn't know what to do. In hindsight it would have been much better to sign with the Leafs, go to the farm club that first year in Oklahoma City at that time, do extremely well, and then come up and make the team the next year. That's probably what would have happened. I never wanted to leave Toronto; it's all I wanted to play for."

In his second season of pro in 1976–77, Boudreau bounced between the Leafs and their CHL farm team, the Dallas Black Hawks, a shared affiliate with Chicago's NHL club by the same name. In Dallas, despite missing a chunk of the season due to a blown-out shoulder and time spent in Toronto, Boudreau led the league in scoring, tallying 37 goals and 71 points in 58 games.

He remained in that pattern, though. After his first season with the Leafs, Boudreau bounced between the NHL club and its affiliate in the CHL and then the AHL in Moncton with the New Brunswick Hawks, Cincinnati with the Tigers, and St. Catharines with the Saints. In six seasons with the team, he played 134 regular season NHL games and nine playoff games, registering a combined 29 goals and 71 points.

"I thought I had a really good opportunity with the Leafs after my first year, but they were just always looking for something more to play behind Darryl Sittler. They got Walt McKechnie, they got Stan Weir, and they got all of these guys thinking they could do the job and then I got sent down and recalled when they realized that those guys were not as good as they thought," Boudreau said.

In his yo-yoing between levels, Boudreau also got to know another player taken among the 17 the Leafs drafted in 1975 (the most picks they've ever made in a single draft). That player was Ron Wilson, a natural defencemen out of Providence College who the Leafs converted to forward after drafting him 132nd in 1975.

It was Wilson, coincidentally, who constantly swapped assignments with him. When Boudreau went up, it normally meant Wilson was coming down. And when Boudreau went down, it normally meant Wilson had received a call to go in the other direction.

Like Boudreau, though, Wilson never filled the void the Leafs teams of the era were looking to fill, playing just 70 NHL games and registering just 26 points in parts of three seasons with the franchise before signing to play in Switzerland and later returning to play another 127 NHL games for the Minnesota North Stars in the late '80s.

"Ron would be incredibly good in today's game on defence, but back then, that smooth-skating, non-physical defenceman, there wasn't a lot of them," Boudreau said. "But he was very, very gifted and very smart. And he went to college, and I went to juniors and in the '70s, juniors knew nothing about college, just as the college guys knew nothing about juniors. So I had no clue who he was and it was later on in life that I realized he was with Brian Burke and Lou Lamoriello and a dozen more people at Providence that became big NHLers."

The seeds of Boudreau's and Wilson's shared passion for coaching were planted in those years together, too.

"The one thing I remember about us is we'd have great talks about hockey and it's just wild that we both ended up doing the same job, because we both loved talking about hockey and ideas," Boudreau said. "It's as simple as that."

When Boudreau felt like he'd gone from "prospect to suspect" into his later years with the Leafs organization, he took that interest in coaching to the higher-ups and they made him a player assistant coach under Cincinnati Tigers head coach Doug Carpenter in 1981–82, a position he continued to hold with the St. Catharines Saints in 1982–83, again under Carpenter (who a decade later became head coach of the Leafs for two seasons). After leaving the Leafs organization in the summer of 1984 and signing with the Blackhawks a year later, Boudreau continued to serve in a similar role with Chicago's farm team, the Nova Scotia Oilers, as a "liaison to the farm club" because Chicago's assistant general manager Jack Davison didn't want to call him a coach and they were splitting the affiliation with Edmonton. With the Nova Scotia Oilers, who were located in Halifax, Boudreau wrote reports on his Chicago teammates, communicating over regular phone calls to update the NHL club on how they were being treated.

"With no cell phones or internet or anything, you didn't really know unless you were there," Boudreau said. "But I still wanted to do the same thing: get into coaching. So I organized all those calls with Chicago."

Into the late '80s, Boudreau remained a top AHL player, winning the league's 1988 scoring title with the Springfield Indians when he posted 116 points in 80 games at age 33. As the '80s turned into the '90s, he continued to serve as a player assistant coach for two more seasons with the Fort Wayne Komets in the IHL, which was then still trying to challenge the AHL as hockey's top minor league.

By the time his career wound down and it was nearly time to retire, Boudreau already had nearly a decade of coaching-adjacent work under his belt, and he knew that he wanted to pursue it as his second career in the sport. After posting 84 points in 77 games with the Komets at age 37, Boudreau entered the summer of 1992 still intent on continuing to play professionally with a résumé that boasted 150 NHL games and more than 1,100 minor league points. But when the Muskegon Fury of the newly formed Central Hockey League approached him to become its first head coach, it gave him pause.

"I wanted to play until I couldn't walk anymore. And my thought was that once you become a veteran in the AHL and the IHL, as soon as you had a bad year, you were done. And I hadn't had a bad year yet, so I was still OK. But I knew that if I had a bad year the next year at 38 years old, maybe there would be no coaching jobs open for me," Boudreau said. "So when this one came and it was a three-year deal, I knew I was going to be employed and I took it."

From there, one job led to another. After one year in Muskegon, Boudreau and former Leafs teammate John Anderson attended the 1993 NHL draft in Quebec City to pursue other coaching jobs. Anderson, after returning to play one more season of pro hockey, used the networking they did at the draft to later get head coaching jobs of his own, climbing the IHL and AHL ranks to become a three-time NHL coach with the Atlanta Thrashers, Phoenix Coyotes, and Minnesota Wild. Boudreau used a conversation with Los Angeles Kings head coach Barry Melrose to leave his three-year contract in Muskegon to return to Fort Wayne, then a Kings farm team, after his former head coach there, Al Sims, was hired as an NHL assistant with the expansion Anaheim Mighty Ducks. After Muskegon and Fort Wayne came a job with the IHL's San Francisco Spiders, another with the ECHL's Mississippi Sea Wolves (a team he led to the minor league's 1999 title), an AHL promotion to the Lowell Lock Monsters, a second AHL gig with the Manchester Monarchs, and then a third with the Hershey Bears, where he led the team to back-to-back AHL finals in 2006 and 2007, winning the Calder Cup in the first. His success with the Bears then prompted a promotion to the NHL when their NHL affiliate, the Washington Capitals, fired their head coach Glen Hanlon after 21 games in 2007–08. In 2009, he was also inducted into the AHL Hall of Fame. After five seasons behind the Capitals bench, Boudreau spent five more with the Anaheim Ducks from 2011 to '16 and another four with the Minnesota Wild from 2016 to '20, before falling out of work for the first time in a decade only to be hired by the Vancouver Canucks in December 2021. With the Canucks, he surpassed 1,000 NHL games coached, charming his new team and its fan base with his folksy demeanour.

In Minnesota, Boudreau hired Anderson as his assistant. He didn't meet Ken Holland, drafted by the Leafs with him and Wilson in 1975, until a recent coaching and management summit he participated in after being let go by the Wild. Holland, a goalie, was drafted after Boudreau and Wilson with the Leafs' 188th overall pick in 1975, but he never played a game within the organization and played in just four NHL games in Hartford and Detroit before working for the Red Wings for 34 years (22 of which were spent as general manager) and more recently, the Oilers, winning three Stanley Cups along the way.

In his life in coaching, Boudreau remained close with Wilson as Wilson climbed the ladder himself with Switzerland's HC Davos, the AHL's Moncton Hawks, and the NHL's Canucks (as an assistant coach under Burke, one of those Providence alums), Mighty Ducks, Capitals, Sharks, and eventually the Maple Leafs, where his two-decade career as an NHL coach ended with three-and-a-half seasons behind Toronto's bench from 2008 to '12 when he was replaced by...1976 Leafs draft pick Randy Carlyle.

RANDY CARLYLE IS chuckling to himself as he recounts how he found out he'd been drafted by the Leafs.

He was at his parents' home in Azilda, a small community just outside of Sudbury, and he was cutting the grass when his mom opened the porch door and called out.

"Hey, you're wanted on the phone!" she shouted.

After leaving the person at the other end of the phone hanging for a few moments while he finished the line of grass he was in the middle of, he sauntered in to find that it was Jim Gregory calling to inform him that the Leafs had selected him with the 30th pick of the draft. Unlike Boudreau's reaction of a year earlier, Carlyle was elated. Back then, NHL fandom was divided entirely by the language you spoke in the highly bilingual Sudbury area. His French-speaking neighbours were Montreal Canadiens fans. His English-speaking neighbours, himself among them, were Maple Leafs fans.

Like Boudreau, he was a top player on a top OHA team. A year after Boudreau's Marlboros had won the OHA title and the Memorial Cup, Carlyle's Sudbury Wolves had lost just 11 of 66 games in the 1976 season, falling to the Hamilton Fincups in the league's final to miss out on a Memorial Cup run of their own. Carlyle was the team's fourth-leading scorer and highest-scoring defenceman, with 79 points in 60 games. Before the Leafs picked him, three of his Wolves teammates—Rod Schutt (13th overall to the Canadiens), Alex McKendry (14th to the Islanders), Dave Farrish (24th to the Rangers)—had already been drafted. Carlyle had no indication that the Leafs were interested in him, though, knowing only where he was ranked by NHL Central Scouting, which was still in its infancy. When scouts had come into town, they would meet with Jerry Toppazzini, the Wolves' head coach and a legend in the area who had scored 407 points in 783 games across 12 NHL seasons in the '50s and '60s, to set up a chat with players. But only the NHL's St. Louis Blues had expressed any serious interest in Carlyle, even though he was a star.

Part of the reason for that was because, like Boudreau, Carlyle's agent betrayed his trust. Carlyle was represented by Art Kaminsky, who all the local players had hired. When Carlyle was selected into the WHA seventh overall by the Cincinnati Stingers and signed a letter of intent to attend the team's training camp in February 1976, a few months before the NHL draft, Kaminsky lied to NHL clubs about it, telling them that he'd signed a contract. So when Carlyle told the Leafs that he was interested in signing straightaway to play in the NHL, they were surprised. The day after their draft day conversation, Jim Gregory, John McLellan, and George Armstrong made the four-hour drive from Toronto to Sudbury's President Hotel to meet with Carlyle and Wolves general manager Joe Drago to offer him a contract, which he took and which prompted him to abruptly end his relationship with Kaminsky.

In Carlyle's first Leafs training camp a few months after the draft in the fall of 1976, he made the opening-night roster as a 20-year-old rookie. But after playing little and playing poorly as a fill-in for superstar Borje Salming, whose face was gruesomely injured and required 250 stitches to reconstruct that November, Carlyle was sent to Dallas in early January, where Boudreau was in the midst of pursuing his goal-scoring title. There, Carlyle formed a quick bond with Boudreau (whom his teammates affectionately called Gabby) and Anderson before he was called back up in late February and played the remainder of the year and into the 1977 playoffs on his own merits.

The next year, things played out in almost identical fashion. Carlyle made the Leafs out of camp, was sent to Dallas in January, and returned in February to finish the regular season and play into the playoffs, helping the Leafs top the Kings and Islanders before falling to the Canadiens in a sweep in the semifinals.

That summer, he got a second draft call from Jim Gregory, this time telling him that his two seasons in Toronto would be his only ones because they'd dealt him to Pittsburgh alongside Leafs forward George Ferguson in exchange for Penguins defenceman Dave Burrows and the 92nd pick in that year's draft (which they used to draft tough guy Mel Hewitt, who never played an NHL game). The trade came as a shock, because Carlyle felt like he'd finished the season strong, but it helped him get to a place that Boudreau never was able to—the top of an NHL lineup—because the Penguins had just missed the playoffs and were short on defenders.

After posting just 20 points in 110 games across two seasons and two playoffs with the Leafs, Carlyle broke out in his first season in Pittsburgh, leading the team's defence in scoring with 47 points in 70 games. He spent the rest of his 17-year NHL career playing for the Penguins and the Jets, winning the Norris Trophy as the league's best defenceman when he registered 83 points in 76 games with the Penguins in 1980–81. In the twilight of his career with the Jets, Carlyle, like Boudreau before him, set his sights on coaching and asked in his final contract negotiation with the team if they'd promise him a job when he retired. When he finally did, retiring with 580 points and more than 1,400 penalty minutes in nearly 1,100 games, the team's owner, Barry Shenkarow, gave him a verbal commitment and a handshake offer for a post-playing career job.

That job became commentary on the radio broadcasts with legendary local announcers Don Whitman and Curt Keilback. After the radio job came a role as the Jets' director of player development and two seasons as an amateur scout with the NHL club.

As a scout with the Jets in the mid-90s, Carlyle developed an appreciation for the job that made him a Leaf all those years earlier and the way it had changed in the years since NHL Central Scouting was its only barometer.

"The scouts are the bird dogs. They're the ones out in the field. And they've got an extremely difficult job. For people who can cast stones in the direction of scouting staffs and say, 'Well, you didn't get this player, or you didn't get that player,' I would just liken it to looking back on some of the decisions those people made in their lives when they were 18 and how much different their decisions would be at 40 years of age, and how different they would look at things," Carlyle said. "Because that's basically what you're trying to do, is you're trying to predict what a 17- or 18-year-old is going to become with all of these outside factors that you have no control over. It's a very unforgiving position. And they put the hours in to go where the players are. There's a lot of sacrificing for those guys, who are always away from their families, and missing birthdays, and missing everything."

Carlyle's first coaching job eventually followed on the Jets bench under head coach Terry Simpson in 1995–96. But when Shenkarow sold the Jets to Phoenix businessman Jerry Colangelo at the end of that season, moving them to Phoenix to become the Coyotes, only general manager John Paddock was kept on staff. In Winnipeg and out of work, Carlyle was hired by Mark Chipman, who had just purchased the IHL's Minnesota Moose and moved them to Winnipeg and, two decades later, brought the Jets back to Winnipeg. Under Chipman, Carlyle progressed from Moose assistant coach to head coach and eventually team president before he got his second NHL opportunity as an assistant with the Capitals in 2002.

By the time Carlyle and Wilson came full circle to go from Leafs draft picks in back-to-back years to one's replacement of the other as the head coach of the team in the winter of 2012, Carlyle had already followed up his job in Washington with six seasons as head coach of the Ducks, where he led the team to a 2007 Stanley Cup. A couple months before he took the Leafs job from Wilson, he was fired by the team and replaced by...Bruce Boudreau.

FROM AMATEUR TO ENTRY AND "BIG DADDY" BOB MCGILL

THE NHL DRAFT only really began to take its modern form in 1980. In 1979, it was renamed the NHL Entry Draft, removing the amateur tag so that NHL clubs, after the WHA had ceased operations, could take players who'd previously played professionally. In 1980, the age criteria became what it is today, allowing NHL teams to draft North American–born players between the ages of 18 and 20 and European players between the ages of 18 and 21. The 1980 NHL Entry Draft also took the draft public, moving it from Montreal's Queen Elizabeth Hotel (and briefly its Mount Royal Hotel in 1973 and the NHL's Montreal offices from 1974 to '77) into the Montreal Forum.

The Leafs arrived in Montreal after capping off a tumultuous season with a losing record and a three-game sweep to the Minnesota North Stars in the first round of the playoffs. They were also without their first-round pick, which had been traded in March 1978 along with Errol Thompson and a 1978 second-round pick for Dan Maloney and Detroit's 1980 second rounder. The Red Wings used the Leafs' first-round pick, which was the 11th overall selection, on Mike Blaisdell, who went on to play 343 NHL games. The Leafs made their first selection of the 1980 draft with Detroit's second round pick at 25th overall, selecting Craig Muni, who played just 19 games for Toronto but went on to play 800 more for six other organizations, winning three Stanley Cups with the Oilers.

Nearby Muni in the crowd sat Bob McGill, a kid from Leduc, Alberta, just outside of Edmonton.

McGill had spent the previous season as a rookie in the WHL with the Victoria Cougars. He didn't even know it was his draft year until he went home at Christmas and got a phone call from a family friend.

"You're ranked by NHL Central Scouting for the draft," he was told.

"What are you talking about?" he answered, unaware that 1980 was the first 18-year-old draft.

McGill, a defenceman who played the 1978–79 season for the Abbotsford Flyers in the Junior A BCJHL, quickly became one of the WHL's toughest players, racking up 230 penalty minutes and 21 points in 70 games, helping to lead the Cougars to a WHL finals defeat.

He had travelled to the draft alone and was only in attendance because several of his Cougars teammates—including

Barry Pederson, Brad Palmer, Len Dawes, Tony Feltrin, Torrie Robertson, and Bob Jansch—were also expected to be picked, and because his agent, Norman Caplan, was a giant in the sport who'd made arrangements for him. (Caplan represented more than a quarter of the league's players before he passed away of a heart attack four years later at age 40.) With Caplan's help, McGill and his Cougars teammates got rooms for the weekend of June 11 at the same hotel where legendary boxer "Sugar" Ray Leonard was staying in advance of his June 20 welterweight "The Brawl in Montreal" title fight against Roberto Duran at Montreal's Olympic Stadium. (Leonard's handler even gave them T-shirts when they bumped into him in the lobby.)

In the days before the draft, McGill met with a few teams for some informal interviews. But by the time it started, and he'd taken his seat in his suit to wait, he didn't have a clue when he would be picked and felt out of his element.

"I knew nothing about the NHL draft. I didn't know a damn thing," McGill said. "I mean, shit, I had just turned 18 in April, so I'm only a couple of months after my 18th birthday. It was kind of a whirlwind."

Palmer's name was the first of the Cougars to be called when the North Stars took him with the 16th pick. Pederson was selected two spots later by the Bruins.

Then, after watching Muni stand up and make his way down to the draft floor to meet with the Leafs, the Capitals were supposed to be up next when a timeout was called. After a few minutes, the silence was interrupted and four of the draft's familiar words were spoken: "There's been a trade."

The Leafs had made a move, acquiring the Capitals' 26th overall pick, prospect Tim Coulis (who never played a game in Toronto), and defencemen Robert Picard (Washington's 1977 third overall pick, who was coming off of back-to-back 50-plus point seasons) for goalie Mike Palmateer and the 55th pick.

Immediately after taking Muni, the Leafs then used their second selection in a row on McGill—much to his surprise, because they weren't one of the teams he'd interviewed with in advance.

After a few short minutes, Leafs assistant to the general manager Gord Stellick then tracked McGill down in the crowd, leading him through the stands to the Leafs' draft table, where he met owner Harold Ballard, general manager Gerry McNamara, and the team's scouts for the first time. The Leafs didn't hand out sweaters at the time, but they gave him a hat and shook his hand, welcoming him to the team.

The following year, McGill returned to Victoria for a second season, posting 41 points and a team-high 295 penalty minutes in 66 games. He closed his junior career winning the WHL title the team had fallen just short of a year earlier.

A few months after that championship, a 19-year-old McGill couldn't believe it when he made the Leafs out of training camp, referring to that era in the organization's history as "a strange time." In Toronto, he was one of *three* teenagers to crack the blue line, along with 18-year-old Jim Benning (whom the Leafs had taken sixth overall that summer and went on to become an NHL scout and executive with the Ducks, Sabres, Bruins, and Canucks), and 19-year-old Fred Boimistruck (who was taken in the third round of the 1980 draft, 16 picks after McGill).

"It was like, 'Come on, who does this?'" McGill said of the Leafs' decision to play three teenage rookies on their blue line. "And we weren't a good team…"

McGill carved out a different niche than Benning and Boimistruck, becoming the Leafs' tough guy. In November of McGill's first season in 1981–82, in the midst of a skid during which the Leafs won just five of their first 23 games, captain Darryl Sittler waived his no-trade clause so that he could be dealt to the Philadelphia Flyers. The Leafs again finished near the bottom of the standings, winning 20 of 80 games for the third-worst record in the league. McGill played 66 of those games, finishing ninth in the league in penalty minutes with 263 (a Leafs rookie record to this day).

McGill went on to play six seasons for the Leafs from 1981 to 1987 in one of the franchise's darkest chapters. After sticking with the Leafs for the entirety of his rookie season, he was demoted to the team's AHL affiliate, the St. Catharines Saints, at Christmas of his second season, remaining there until a call-up after the trade deadline in his third year.

In St. Catharines, McGill joined Boimistruck, who'd been demoted just before he had in November 1982.

There he earned his nickname "Big Daddy" Bob McGill, which stuck with him for the remainder of his career and into his life after it. The nickname was given to him by Saints teammate Marc Magnan, a fellow tough guy out of Western Canada who was a 10th-round pick of the Leafs in 1981 and who had gone toe-to-toe with McGill in the WHL. Magnan was reading a book on "Big Daddy" Gene Lipscomb, who was said to be the toughest player to ever play in the NFL at the time, and one night, after McGill had dropped the gloves in the final minutes of a period (which meant that he was sent to the dressing room instead of the penalty box), Magnan sprinted into the room at intermission shouting the same three words over and over again.

"Big Daddy McGill! Big Daddy McGill!" Magnan screamed to laughs from his teammates.

When Magnan made a habit of shouting that every time he passed by McGill at the rink...or whenever he did well in a fight...or any time he entered the room or the team bus, it stuck.

McGill returned full-time to the Leafs in 1984 and remained in the NHL for another decade, playing more than 700 games and finishing his career with a combined 1,854 penalty minutes between the regular season and the playoffs.

He was traded to the Blackhawks on September 3, 1987, along with former Leafs captain Rick Vaive and Steve Thomas for star forward Eddie Olczyk (Chicago's third overall selection in the 1984 draft) and veteran winger Al Secord.

McGill's selection by the Leafs in the second round of the 1980 draft wasn't his only draft experience. When the NHL expanded in 1991 and 1992, he was drafted twice in its expansion drafts, first by the San Jose Sharks (who traded him to the Red Wings) and then a year later by the Tampa Bay Lightning. After a contract dispute with the Lightning, McGill asked for his release in the fall of 1992 and returned to the Leafs for one season before retiring a couple years later.

In retirement, McGill briefly pursued coaching, serving as an assistant in the AHL with the Hershey Bears for two seasons (where he won the 1997 Calder Cup), the head coach of the ECHL's Baton Rouge Kingfish for two seasons, and the head coach of the OHL's Oshawa Generals for one campaign. He also worked eight years as a scout for the WHL's Edmonton Oil Kings, his hometown team.

Today's Leafs fan probably knows "Big Daddy" Bob McGill best for his appearances at community events, all the times he has laced up his skates in Leafs alumni and charity games, and his roles as the team's longtime colour commentator for Toronto Marlies games and analyst with the Leafs Nation Network (formerly Leafs TV). He was hired by the TV arm of the franchise in 2005 and stayed with them until he decided to take a step back and slow down in 2021.

After fighting nearly 150 times in the NHL, McGill faced his toughest fight on May 31, 2017. He was at his cottage just outside of Peterborough, Ontario, when his wife Mary recognized that something wasn't right with him, racing him 3 kilometres to the end of the road—and to cell service—to call 911. They met an ambulance halfway to the Peterborough Regional Health Centre, the nearest hospital, and learned that he had suffered a stroke. He suffered a second stroke in hospital, both of which were linked to a blood clot, and the latter impaired his speech.

He spent the summer of 2017 working to get back to himself through daily rehab. In September, as the Leafs and Marlies returned for their training camp, he returned to work—and the broadcast booth—insistent on keeping his life "business as usual."

"I think that doing the hockey stuff was pretty helpful in keeping my mind sharp and working because of having to go over statistics and do different things to keep your brain working," McGill said. "At the end of the day, I think I've pretty much made a full recovery. Touch wood. I've got lots of living left to do yet. I have to give props to my wife, Mary. She said, 'We're getting in the car and we're going to the hospital.' I think that I'm very fortunate that we got to the hospital when we did."

In 2018, a year after his strokes, McGill and his mom, Kay, who was the first woman to head the Leduc Minor Hockey Association in 1977, were inducted into Leduc's Sports Hall of Fame.

When he looks back on his career, he sighs, remembering how differently things turned out for him than they did for Boimistruck and pointing to how fickle NHL careers really are, even for two kids who were picked one after the other, started their lives together with the Leafs at the same age, and were demoted a month apart.

"I got called up and stayed in the NHL pretty much the rest of my career. But Freddie never recovered from it. He never played another game of hockey in the NHL again. He played a third year and then he was done. It's crazy how things turn out," McGill said.

Through his role with the Leafs' broadcast team, and specifically the Marlies, he also watched firsthand as the draft process and the young players entering their own pro careers both changed.

"When you look at the way things have changed today and the whole production of what goes on at the draft, it's so, so different," McGill said. "The whole draft process leading up to it now with the combine, it has become way more scientific as far as the teams are concerned with how they go about researching the players. And the kids today are so well prepared. When you have a conversation with them, the agents have schooled these kids and taught them what to say so much that it's almost robotic."

The day itself hasn't changed, though. The handshake introductions, the hat, the butterflies, and that out-of-your-element feeling? McGill's certain that's the same.

"At the end of the day, it's a pretty special day in your life. It's something that you'll never forget," McGill said. "Having your name called by an NHL team, and especially the Leafs, there's nothing like it."

5

THE DEFECTIONS
OF THE IHNACAK
BROTHERS

A **S PETER IHNACAK** stepped out of his taxi with his brother John, surveyed the docks below, and got in line to board the 16-hour ferry trip from Helsinki to Stockholm, he knew that the rest of his life sat in the balance of the next few minutes.

A quick glance over his papers and the punching of his ticket came with a chance—and only a chance—to apply for political asylum in Sweden and make his way to North America, where the Maple Leafs had promised they'd select him in the 1982 NHL Draft. But any thorough review of his documents would flag that he wasn't permitted to travel without the Eastern Bloc's approval—and he did *not* have approval.

As the line inched closer to the ramp between the dock and the boat, his heart raced. He tried to act normal, but he couldn't help but peek his head out of the queue to carefully watch the officer in front of him check each passenger's papers. Just before they arrived at the front of the line, John began to panic.

"You know what, we are fucked," John said. "I think we should go back to the hotel."

But before they could change their minds, it was their turn and the officer spoke.

"Tickets," he said, extending his hand as John scrambled nervously to pull them out of his pocket.

PETER IHNACAK'S STORY before that moment, before John handed over their papers and waited for the officer to wave them through or pause, was a slow build to a life-changing endeavour.

Peter was born in Poprad, Czechoslovakia, as the third of four children along with his older brother, John; older sister, Magda; and younger brother, Miroslav. He didn't start playing hockey until he was 13 years old but fell in love with the sport almost instantly, and his knack for it followed. Each day when school finished at 2 PM, he rushed home, gathered his equipment, and made his way to the rink, where he'd often practice for seven hours before returning home by midnight.

In those days, he never imagined that the better he got, the more trapped he would become. But that's exactly what happened.

After starring for Czechoslovakia on home ice at the 1977 World Juniors, where he posted seven points in as many games en route to a bronze medal win over the Finns, Peter quickly became a star. The season after the world juniors, he made his professional debut with ASD Dukla Jihlava. A year after that he was recruited to play for TJ Sparta CKD Praha in Prague, where he immediately became the team's leading scorer.

And when Czechoslovakia's national team travelled east to play tournaments in the Soviet Union, East Germany, Poland, or Romania, he always played. But when it went west, it left him behind.

At first, officials came up with excuses for why he wasn't allowed to participate. In 1980, just before his flight to Lake Placid to represent Czechoslovakia at the Winter Olympics, they used the Soviet invasion of Afghanistan as their reason. (The Soviets had deployed their military across the border on December 24, 1979, a month and a half before the Games.)

"The situation is dangerous and we can't let you go," he was told.

Eventually, though, the excuses made way for the truth, which was that they felt he was a flight risk for the NHL, which had just begun to recruit and draft European players in larger numbers. After playing at the top of the Czechoslovakia lineup in a December 1980 tournament in Russia, they took him off the team in advance of an upcoming one in January. Before the 1981 Canada Cup, after he was told he'd made the national team in camp, a pair of KGB agents boarded the team's flight and told him they were investigating him for defection, and he wouldn't be allowed to leave the country.

In the 1981–82 season after the September Canada Cup, things eventually came to a head between Peter and communist authorities when he was planning a trip to Germany with a couple of teammates and he received a call from Sparta Praha's secretary.

"After practice, come to the office. There are some guys that want to talk to you," she told him.

Following his post-practice shower, he was greeted by five KGB agents in suits, his eyes widening.

"Yeah, what's wrong?" he asked them.

"Mr. Ihnacak, you want to travel to Germany?" one of the men answered.

"Yeah."

"Bad luck, give us your passport, you won't be travelling anywhere."

"OK," he said, knowing he didn't have a choice as they ushered him to their car and drove him back to his apartment in search of his papers.

When he couldn't immediately find his passport in his apartment, Peter told the authorities that his girlfriend had it in an effort to buy himself some time.

"Tomorrow, bring the passport to the police station," they told him.

That night, he stirred in his apartment, sleepless, debating whether or not he should try to hop on a bus or train to leave the country but fearful that if he did he'd be stopped at the border and put himself in even more trouble.

The following day, he caved, handing over his passport to authorities. A week later, he received a letter in the mail that stated he was an "enemy of the state" and could not be trusted to own travel documents. Outraged, he quit playing for Sparta Praha in protest, hopeful that he'd be given his

paperwork back and allowed to travel with the club team—
and his national team.

"Listen to me, if I'm a normal citizen then I would be able
to travel, but because I play hockey and you are the ones that
I travel with, you won't let me," he said on a joint call with
authorities and team staff.

When another letter followed, this time telling him that
he'd missed 10 consecutive days of work and he could be
arrested, tried, and jailed for his refusal to play, Peter had no
choice but to return to the team.

That spring, when the season was over, he again attended
Czechoslovakia's camp for the 1982 World Championships,
which were set to be held in Helsinki, expecting he wouldn't
be allowed to participate.

Finally, though, a combination of things worked in his
favour.

The first was that several of the national team's staff for
the 1982 World Championships also happened to work for
the two clubs he'd played on in Prague and Jihlava, and they
were willing to try to convince Soviet officials to let him participate. The second was his play itself. When they left him off
the Canada Cup squad, the line he was supposed to play on
performed poorly and by the time the world championships
rolled around, he was a 24-year-old who'd already proven he
was one of the country's top players in four full seasons with
Sparta Praha, so there were selfish reasons for *them* to let *him*
help chase a gold medal.

The deciding factor, though, was Finland's more restrictive immigration rules than the countries he had previously

been prohibited from travelling to, which Soviet officials knew would prevent him from trying to both stay *or* leave.

"They took me to Finland because in Finland they didn't accept immigrants. I knew that," Peter said. "I didn't have a passport, I didn't have a visa, I didn't have anything. And if I disappeared and showed up at a Finnish police station to say, 'I want to stay here and apply for political asylum,' they'd say, 'No, we have to return you back to Prague.'"

In Helsinki, Peter quickly called John, who was living in New York after leaving Czechoslovakia in 1968, nearly a decade and a half earlier, with Magda.

"John, I'm in Finland and I don't want to go back," he told his brother.

"Be quiet, don't tell anybody, and in a couple of days I will come to Finland and I will help you out," John answered, promising to book a flight and pretend like he was travelling over as a fan to watch the tournament.

At the airport, John then recognized Leafs head coach Mike Nykoluk and general manager Gerry McNamara and approached them to chat. They told him that they were travelling over to Europe to scout someone to help Miroslav Frycer (who'd defected a year earlier from Czechoslovakia to the Nordiques before a trade deadline move to the Leafs) adjust. John trusted the two brasses with his brother's story and told them to keep an eye on him. After watching Peter play early in the tournament, Nykoluk and McNamara then arranged a secret meeting with John, presenting him with a pre-emptive contract (which would today be considered tampering) and promising to draft Peter if he could successfully escape, with John serving as a translator for his brother, who spoke no English.

"He has to stay quiet so that nobody knows where he is because if others find out that he's coming over then in the summer there's the possibility that they're going to pick him in the NHL draft," McNamara told John.

John spent the day after their conversation with the Leafs looking into exit options while Peter practiced with the national team. Knowing that his brother would never get through pass control at the airport, he turned his attention to the nearby harbour and eventually the ferry (an overnight trip which was a favourite of partying locals and tourists) to Stockholm, where he knew the Swedes' immigration rules were more amenable to those running from the Soviet regime.

That night, John rang Peter in his hotel room.

"Tomorrow, 5 PM, I'm waiting in the taxi behind the hotel. Come, don't take anything, leave everything behind and just take the documents that you have and your toothbrush and toothpaste," John said.

Peter told him he'd be there, and he was, defecting mid-tournament. The officer at the entrance waved them through and they spent the night on the boat before landing the next morning in Sweden. As they stepped off, local media were already there, having caught wind of his run for it overnight, snapping pictures and shouting at him.

Their first trip was a rushed cab ride to the Canadian embassy in Stockholm, where they were told that Peter could apply for immigration status but he would have to wait as many as seven months in Sweden for the paperwork to be completed. Knowing they couldn't afford to wait and that they were likely being followed, John then made a second visit to the United States embassy.

"We are in danger here, we don't know what can happen, and Canada says he has to apply from outside the country," John pleaded.

The U.S. embassy told them they'd get in touch with the White House and see what they could do. After they had hidden out for one night in Stockholm, the American embassy managed to make arrangements for Peter, securing him a visa and helping him get a flight to New York with McNamara.

In New York, the first thing Peter did was track down a copy of *The Hockey News* at a stand outside Madison Square Garden.

"I was looking for a picture because I wanted to see guys naked to see how big they are and how they look because I had no idea," Peter said, having never watched NHL hockey or been to North America.

He spent the summer in New York waiting for his immigration status to come through in Canada and laying low so that he didn't lose out on the guarantees the Leafs had made to him.

"That contract was security to me," Peter said. "I couldn't do anything to screw it up."

He turned 25 that May, a couple weeks after making the trip, and settled into a rigorous routine to pass the time. He'd wake up at 6 AM to get a run in, come back to John's apartment, eat breakfast, go to the gym until noon, return to the apartment for lunch, nap, and then go for a second run each evening. Back at home, the KGB moved swiftly to punish Miroslav for his big brother's decision, preventing him from travelling outside the Soviet Union.

"My immigration destroyed my brother because he couldn't travel anywhere. Like, he was done. I mean, they took *all* of his stuff," Peter said.

The early days of the move crushed Peter, too. He constantly second-guessed his decision, he couldn't communicate with anyone other than his brother because of the language barrier, and he worried about his family.

"It was a shock. I left everything behind. It wasn't easy to digest. It was unbelievably hard," Peter said.

The Leafs came through at the 1982 draft in Montreal, though. After taking Gary Nylund third overall and Gary Leeman 24th, the Leafs used the 25th pick of the draft to select Peter. They also took a chance on Miroslav, then 20 and five years younger than his brother, selecting him seven rounds later with the 171st pick even though they knew taking him would only make his own attempts to leave near impossible.

Peter was finally able to make his way to Toronto in September, just in time for Leafs training camp. Though he couldn't communicate with anyone other than Frycer when he got there, he was surprised by how many people knew him (something he later realized was because the second-round pick that was used on him was part of the trade that sent captain Darryl Sittler to Philadelphia, which made fans particularly invested in his play).

"When I was at the airport, I went through customs and the guy says, 'Hey Peter, good luck, everything's going to be good,' and everywhere I went it was unbelievable. When I was in Europe, I was good at hockey and nobody knew who I was. But there, it was big publicity," Peter said.

In his first season in Toronto, in part because of his age, he stepped right into Nykoluk's lineup and finished third on the team in scoring with 66 points in 80 games, a Leafs rookie scoring record that remained until Auston Matthews narrowly broke it in 2017.

In the decade that followed before the Velvet Revolution of 1989 restored democracy in Czechoslovkia and the 1993 dissolution and separation of the country into the Czech Republic and the Slovak Republic, Peter never saw his family. In August 1983, between his rookie and sophomore seasons with the Leafs, his father, Stefan, passed of cancer and he wasn't able to say goodbye.

"I just kind of talked to him on the phone and then the last few weeks, he couldn't even talk. I heard his breathing on the phone on the other side, but he couldn't speak anymore and I couldn't go to the funeral," Peter said. "It broke my heart."

The only comfort he found was in his new home.

"I wanted to become as soon as possible Canadian. I love Canada. I love the people," Peter said. "I wanted to adjust as much as possible to the Canadian way of living, to learn English as soon as possible. It's the best country in the world."

While his brother played for the Leafs, Miroslav became an even better player than Peter with HC Kosice, leading Czechoslovakia's professional league in scoring with 35 goals and 66 points in 43 games in 1984–85.

For a couple of years, Miroslav tried to find legal ways to leave with the Leafs' help.

"One way was that he would marry somebody from the West or from Yugoslavia and then they found a girl in

Yugoslavia who would marry him but the communists said no. He was, like, locked," Peter said of his brother's efforts.

Eventually, just after Christmas and in the middle of the 1985–86 season, with Miroslav sitting atop the league's scoring race for a second straight year with 32 points through the first 21 games, the Leafs paid a diplomat to invite him to Bratislava, at the country's border with Austria, and smuggle him to Vienna.

Miroslav, then 23, showed up to his meeting with his girlfriend, Eva, not knowing anything about the arrangements that had been made. Together, the pair agreed to take sleeping pills and be loaded into the trunk of a car that had been outfitted with stronger shocks to help cushion the 70-kilometre ride between Bratislava and Vienna. They woke up on the other side, where McNamara had flown in to meet them by way of Linzer and a two-hour bus ride when his flight into Vienna was diverted due to gunfire at the airport.

In Vienna, the Canadian consulate told Miroslav, Eva, and McNamara that they would have to apply for asylum at an Austrian refugee camp before they could be granted immigration papers to Canada, a process which would reportedly take two months. All three, fearful that they were being shadowed and could be apprehended by Soviet officials, eventually got the help of two Canadian cabinet ministers when they leaked their cries for help to Canadian and American news media.

Together, the trio then caught the first flight they could out of the country, a roundabout route that took them the long way around the globe to Vancouver. Peter got a call from McNamara with the news when they landed.

"We're getting a red eye plane to Toronto," McNamara told him, to tears of joy.

On January 4, 1986, Miroslav was introduced in a press conference in Toronto alongside Peter, who served as his translator, McNamara, and owner Harold Ballard, who gloated, "Any communist that I could get out of there that wanted to be a Canadian, I'm very pleased," and denied reports of the money he had spent to secure Miroslav's escape (reports Peter confirmed for this book), crediting "intermediaries" for their help.

Though McNamara and Ballard raved about the impact Miroslav would have on their Leafs, who'd won just 10 of 35 games to that point in the season, Miroslav never had the NHL career his brother did. He and Eva moved in with Peter for the first couple of months, but he found the adjustment harsher than his brother had.

"He was in shock. I had this advantage because I came in April to the U.S. and I had five months to prepare like crazy. Miroslav, he didn't practice or play, and he wasn't ready. He just got off the plane and the next day he was playing with new equipment, new skates," Peter said. "It's too bad things went the way that they went because he was a good hockey player. He needed some help, adjustment time, but the big publicity and the expectations were humongous, and everyone was expecting a superstar. Not a player but a superstar."

Peter went on to play eight seasons for the Leafs, amassing 267 points in 417 games. Miroslav bounced between the Leafs and their farm team in St. Catharines and then Newmarket, playing just 55 NHL games for the team across three seasons before finishing his short-lived career in North America with a one-game stint with the Red Wings and three more years in the AHL in Adirondack and Halifax.

When their NHL pursuits were over, both brothers spent the 1990s playing in Germany and Switzerland. Peter retired from the Krefeld Penguins in 1997 at age 40. Miroslav spent the early 2000s playing professionally in Slovakia, returning to Kosice HC for five seasons before retiring in 2006 at the age of 44. In retirement, Miroslav took up coaching and has led professional teams in Slovakia, Poland, Hungary, and Italy. Peter coached a trio of teams in the DEL, Germany's top professional league, before the Leafs hired him as a European amateur scout in 2005. He was let go by the Leafs in 2015 when president Brendan Shanahan took over the club and cleaned house, but Peter remained active in alumni games. Today, he has finally moved back to Prague, where he scouts the Czech Republic and its neighbouring countries for the Washington Capitals, who hired him in 2016.

Toronto will always feel closer to home than home does.

"It was difficult, but I had an unbelievable time with the Maple Leafs," Peter said. "I'm happy that it happened when it happened."

6

TORONTO'S FIRST DRAFT...AND FIRST NO. 1 PICK

AFTER THE NHL draft went public in 1980, it was only a matter of time until it left Montreal for the first time, too. In 1984, in its fifth straight year at the Montreal Forum, the draft was broadcast live for the first time when the Canadian Broadcasting Corporation (CBC) aired it in both English and French to a Canada-only audience.

A year later, when the draft began its since-familiar circuit around the league to new host cities each June, the 1985 NHL draft marked a pair of firsts for the Maple Leafs. Not only did they get to host for the first time, welcoming 7,000 fans into the Metro Toronto Convention Centre (conveniently located just down the street from the CBC's studios) for the one-day event, but it was also the first time in the draft's then-23-year history that the Leafs were set to pick first overall. The slotting came after they ended the 1984–85 season in last place in the 21-team league, winning just 20 of 80 games to finish with 48 points (five fewer than the next-worst Penguins). In the audience sat a 5'11", tough-as-nails defenceman from Kelvington, Saskatchewan. He was wearing a tan suit and navy-blue pants, his sandy blond mullet tucked long behind his ears and matched by an unmistakable, thick mustache.

His name was Wendel Clark.

CLARK ARRIVED AT the 1985 draft by way of a blue-collar hockey upbringing that informed the player he'd become. That upbringing started on the Clark family's cattle and grain farm just outside of Kelvington, a rural town of fewer than 1,000 people—where his father, Les, was also born—located more than two and a half hours east of Saskatoon. He was born in 1966 as the middle of three Clark boys to older brother Donn (born in 1962) and younger brother Kerry (born in 1968).

Hockey ran in the blood, the water, and everything else. Kerry became a 10th-round pick of the Islanders in 1986 and racked up 2,812 penalty minutes in 10 seasons split between the minor league AHL and IHL. After four seasons as an in-and-out-of-the-lineup type in the WHL, Donn spent 17 seasons on the other side of the sport as a head coach and general manager in the league, leading the Prince Albert Raiders and Saskatoon Blades in the 1990s and 2000s. Several sets of the Clark family's cousins were also born and raised in Kelvington and went on to have careers in hockey. Wendel's uncle, Jim Melrose, ran the local rink and raised one of

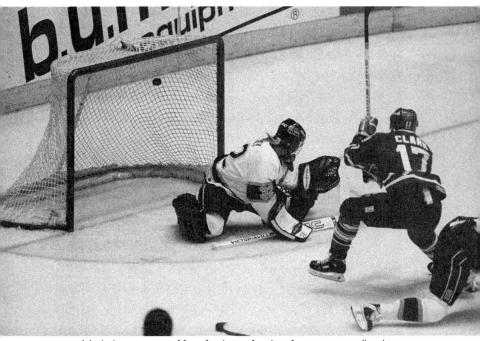

Wendel Clark was a man of firsts for the Leafs—their first No. 1 overall pick. The first pick of the first draft held in Toronto. And eventually, he was traded for another first overall pick: Mats Sundin. *(AP Photo/Mark J. Terrill)*

his children, Barry, to become a second-round pick of the Montreal Canadiens (and a Leaf for three seasons in the early 1980s). On the other side of the family, two different sets of Kelvington's Kocur family raised Wendel's cousins Joey (a fifth-round pick of the Red Wings in 1983 who won three Stanley Cups with the team) and Kory (a first-round pick of the Red Wings in 1988 who never made it to the NHL).

In time, Wendel came to eclipse each of them.

First there was AAA hockey in Yorkton, 150 kilometres south of Kelvington, at age 13 and 14, which required leaving directly from school and not returning home until after midnight just to attend practices. Then there was the Notre Dame Hounds AAA team in Wilcox, a further three hours south of Kelvington, at age 15 and 16. And by the time he'd followed in Kerry and Donn's footsteps to the Saskatoon Blades in the WHL, Wendel was destined for somewhere they never were—the NHL.

As a kid and young teenager, though, Wendel's sights were never really set on the NHL. Things only began to change around Christmas of his first season in Saskatoon when he found out that he was ranked by NHL Central Scouting. When the calendar changed from 1983 to 1984, Wendel began fielding calls and in-person meetings with NHL clubs every second day in the New Year. And when his rookie year was over, he'd posted 68 points and 225 penalty minutes in 72 games, stamping his mythic heart-on-his-sleeve style.

Early on in Wendel's sophomore season, his agent, Norm Caplan, passed suddenly of a heart attack in late October. Instead of signing on with another agent, he elected to play out the year, his draft year, without representation so that he could focus on his play.

"I just played and stayed out of the politics of it," a 54-year-old Clark said with his typical succinctness on a phone call in the spring of 2021.

His strategy worked when he registered a further 93 points and racked up another 260 penalty minutes in a combined 67 games between the regular season and the playoffs to finish second on the team in scoring, first in penalty minutes, and among the league's leaders in both categories for a defenceman. He also represented Canada at the 1985 World Juniors in Helsinki and Turku, Finland, scoring three goals and five points in seven games en route to a gold medal win over Czechoslovakia. Eventually, when his draft year was done and his Blades had been swept in three games by the Regina Pats in the first round of the 1985 WHL playoffs, Wendel joined agent Don Meehan and his Newport Sports Management (which he'd started four years earlier and today represents more than 100 NHL players). In the run-up to the draft, though he knew he would likely be picked inside the top three, Wendel had no idea whether he'd be picked first.

As he made his way down through the crowd and was handed his Maple Leafs jersey by Leafs staffer Gord Stellick, sportscaster Don Wittman greeted him at the draft floor to interview him as he walked toward the Leafs' draft table.

Clark answered Wittman's questions curtly and almost nonchalantly, a sign of things to come in the way he would carry himself through the rest of his career in Toronto.

"What do you think you'll be able to add to the Toronto Maple Leafs?"

"I just hope to do my best and hope to help the club," Clark said as they arrived at the table, removing his jacket and pulling his new jersey over his head.

On the broadcast, the team assembled in Toronto to cover the event responded with a bit of surprise, believing the Leafs would take defenceman Dana Murzyn.

More than three and a half decades later, Clark confesses he didn't know he'd be their pick either.

"The Leafs didn't tip their hand, or they didn't tip it to me at all. But boy was it neat to get picked first overall, and at the draft in Toronto," Wendel said of the eventual name-call, describing a blur of tables, fan excitement, and frenzied interview stops.

His memories of the days that followed come into focus a little clearer because the next thing he knew he was leaving the province he'd called home his entire life to move to Scarborough, bordering Toronto's east end, and bunk in with the parents of Peter Zezel, another of Meehan's clients who no longer lived at home and was entering his second season with the Flyers.

Then, on his first day of camp, Wendel arrived to a surprise.

"I read my name on the door and it said, 'left wing, Wendel Clark.' That's how it started. As simple as that," he said with a chuckle of the move from defence to forward, a move he'd briefly made with Team Canada at the world juniors because it was the only way he'd make the team but not one he expected to make in the NHL.

Nonetheless, Wendel became a shot in the arm for a team that sorely needed one. He turned 19 at the end of October, a few weeks into his rookie season, went to the All-Star game (his first of two career appearances), and led the Leafs in goals (34) and penalty minutes (227). At Maple Leaf Gardens, he quickly became a fan favourite as a teenager, a bond that he says began to form on day one with his new team.

"A lot of me starting to get the fans on my side probably started with the draft because it was in Toronto. You had a relationship that kicked off in June before the season started," Wendel said. "And the style of game that people liked wasn't any different whether you were in junior or the NHL. I played the same style I'd played at every level. That was an exciting style for a fan to watch."

With Wendel always in the thick of things, the Leafs took a modest step forward, finishing fourth in the five-team Norris Division (which was still one of their worst records as a franchise to that point) before stunning the top-seeded Blackhawks with a first-round sweep and falling to the Blues in a tightly-contested seven-game series in the second round. Clark scored five goals and added 47 minutes in the box across their 10 games. When it was over, he finished second in Calder Trophy voting for the league's rookie of the year.

The following season, as a sophomore, he was named an assistant captain before his 20th birthday. Five years after that, he became the Original Six franchise's 14th captain. Though a cross-check to the back against the Blackhawks in 1987 left him hobbled for much of the rest of his storied career, Wendel remained the favourite of the Maple Leaf Gardens crowd into the early 1990s, playing the first nine years of his NHL career in Toronto. In 1992–93, he led the Leafs to a then record 44 wins and 99 points before infamously losing to Wayne Gretzky's Kings, coached by none other than his cousin Barry Melrose, in the Clarence Campbell Conference Finals. His playoff performance that year lives on as one of the Leafs' all-time greats, with 20 points in 21 games and a hat trick in Game 6 in Los Angeles. The following year, in the last of those nine seasons and despite continued injury troubles, Clark scored 55 goals split between 82 regular season and playoff games, a run of play that remains one of the most prolific in franchise history.

That summer, at the 1994 NHL draft, he was dealt to the Quebec Nordiques as part of the blockbuster trade that brought another first overall pick, Mats Sundin, to Toronto. The Leafs never could really get rid of him, though. He was traded back to the team at the 1996 trade deadline with Islanders teammate Mathieu Schneider and prospect D.J. Smith (who two decades later became an assistant coach of the Leafs for four seasons) in exchange for journeymen Darby Hendrickson, Kenny Jonsson, Sean Haggerty, and the Leafs' 1997 first-round pick (which became a fourth overall pick and was used by the Islanders to select future star goalie Roberto Luongo). After spending two more seasons with the Leafs and signing with the Tampa Bay Lightning in the 1998 off-season, Wendel was later released by the Blackhawks in January 2000 and signed to return to the Leafs for a third time in the twilight of his career. In the postseason of that year, he captured the Leafs faithful once more, this time in their new home at the Air Canada Centre, prompting a series of standing ovations en route to a second-round defeat to the eventual Stanley Cup–winning Devils before retiring at age 34.

He finished his Leafs career with 441 points in 608 regular season games and another 61 points in 79 playoff games. In 2008, Clark's No. 17 was raised to the rafters in a November ceremony at the Air Canada Centre. In 2016, it was formally retired in an October ceremony that saw all the Leafs' other previously honoured numbers retired alongside his. In 2017, the Leafs honoured him once more in a teary-eyed unveiling of his statute (one of just 14) on Legends Row in Maple Leaf Square, at the arena's southwest corner. Since the end of his playing days, Wendel has remained a staple of the Leafs' alumni box at home games and on the ice in alumni games as a community ambassador.

Even through some of the organization's most trying years, Wendel never resented being picked first overall or anything that came with it.

"It's no pressure. That's what you've dreamed of your whole life. I don't consider that pressure. Especially your first year, you're 18 years old, you've basically just left high school, and now you're in the NHL," Wendel said. "The whole first year is kind of a blur anyways because there [are] no bad days. You can get injured, and it's a bump in the road, but you're playing in the NHL as a teenager. Whether you have a good season or a bad season, you didn't know how good you were going to be at the highest level anyway. That's my take on it. I simplify it right down to that."

When he reflects on his days on the ice with the Leafs, a couple of things stick with him. The first, he argues, is that some of his teams were better than they get credit for.

"It wasn't evident in the points, but talent-wise that team from 1985 to 1987 had as much skill and talent as the team in 1993. But [it wasn't] put together yet," he'll tell you.

The second is all those special nights at the Gardens (as a Leaf and an opponent) before the Leafs' 67-year tradition in the iconic arena ended in February 1999.

"Visiting teams couldn't wait to play in Toronto in those days. And Toronto was the hardest home team to be because there were always half a dozen players on the other team from Ontario who loved coming home to play," Wendel said. "The Gardens, in that era, Gretzky coming in with the best team ever, [Dale] Hawerchuk coming in as a Toronto guy who always had 100-plus points, there was always, in those high-scoring years, big guys coming in to try to have a big night on national TV with all of their buddies in the stands. That was the best."

But these days, as he watches the Leafs' second first overall pick, Auston Matthews, make new history of his own in Toronto, Wendel still scoffs at the idea that the gig is some kind of a burden.

"The Matthews, the [Mitch] Marners, the [William] Nylanders, when people say, 'Oh, there's all this pressure,' I don't think that's pressure," he said.

For a while, when he and Matthews bumped into each other around the rink, Wendel viewed him as a kid and tried to impart him with advice however he could. Now, whenever they see each other, Wendel sees Matthews as an adult and guidance makes way for laughs. He has cherished watching Matthews find himself in the spotlight, just like he eventually did in Toronto. He remembers when Matthews first arrived, the smiling, soft, easygoing look he always had on his face on the bench, and the way it juxtaposed the coach's intensity behind him. It was the same look he remembers he and teammate Russ Courtnall had in their early days as the Leafs' young stars in the mid-1980s.

"You'd look at their faces and you could tell he and Mitch were still teenagers. And as they've matured now, they carry themselves differently and you can tell their focus has shifted on the bench. And that's just learning it as you play. You can't get told. It's how you pick it up," Wendel said. "Auston has learnt by watching other players."

Some of that maturity is physical, the kind that comes with age and muscle, too. Wendel always had to play bigger than he was to compensate for his size and scrap for his ice. Matthews, he thinks, shied away from that early on. Not anymore.

"When he first came in, he couldn't outmuscle you even though he looked big at 6'3". That happens at 22, 23. It's tough for an 18-year-old to be good in an 82-game schedule against men. So then you go, 'How come he had a bad week?' and it's not because he's hurt per se, but he is under the weather, he's tired. And he can't even tell you that because he's never been through it before," Wendel said. "The first couple of years he was beating you on skill. Now he can beat you on skill and strength. Now he's a hard guy to handle if you're a defenceman."

Wendel has been through the draft process twice now, as well. In 2018, his son Kody proved that maybe it was the Clark blood more than the Kelvington water when he was selected 47th overall by the Capitals out of the OHL's Ottawa 67's. Before the 67's, Wendel coached Kody's AAA Toronto Nationals in the GTHL. Growing up, he often told Kody the same thing he told himself about staying out of hockey's politics. He played the parents of Kody's teammates as straight as he did his teammates and opponents as a player.

"Just play. You can't do anything about the outside," he'd always tell anyone who'd listen.

That, he thinks, is getting harder and harder for the sport's kids and their families to do in today's NHL draft landscape.

"Everybody thinks you've got to lobby to do this and that, in the Toronto area especially. I say to people, 'Hey, I went first overall and my second-to-last game in junior we lost 18–3.' You're not getting judged for that. However many shifts you're getting, you just have to play your best. And they don't understand it, and the parents don't," Wendel said. "If you're a professional scout watching it, you're watching for details that the parents aren't and don't understand what they're looking for. The NHL game has nothing to do with junior hockey or minor hockey. It's another thing."

Kody, he insists, was the perfect case study in how the draft has changed in those ways—and how much harder it has become to project from one level to the next.

"We all see players that come along who were average in junior and really good professionals. Kody never hit puberty until 19. He was a 5'8" starting junior and he's 6'2" now. So you get drafted at 18 but I tell parents that only the phenoms, only the Matthews and the Marners and Nylanders make it. The rest of the NHL doesn't make it until they're 23," Wendel finished. "And more today than in my day."

You won't find first overall picks without agents these days. You won't see first overall picks changing positions in their rookie season these days, either.

7

THE GORD STELLICK YEARS AND THE BELLEVILLE BULLS DRAFT

SCOTT THORNTON HAS just finished pulling a delivery van out of the ditch in front of his home on the outskirts of Collingwood, Ontario, when he steps inside and fields a phone call. He's out of breath and panting, his hands covered in grease from the chain he'd attached to the back of his truck, when the voice on the other end of the line speaks.

"How on earth did it happen?" he's asked, knowing exactly what *it* is.

"There were rumours that there was a good bar in Belleville that they all just got stuck at," Thornton answers, chuckling.

"But having played in Belleville for three years, I don't recall any good bars there, so that can't have been a true story."

Later that afternoon, Steve Bancroft answers the phone from his home in Madoc, Ontario. He tells a different story. "The joke was that the scouting staff for the Leafs was on a limited budget and could only get as far as Belleville," he says, laughing.

A day after that, Danny Flynn picks up a phone from his home in Greater Lakeburn, New Brunswick, explaining that he remembers seeing then Leafs scouts George Armstrong and Doug Woods around Belleville's Yardmen Arena *a lot* because his Bulls were one of the only teams in the OHL that played on Wednesdays, and there was nowhere else for them to be.

After Bancroft, Thornton, and Flynn, a fourth person fields the same question, this time from Toronto. His name is Gord Stellick, and he was the general manager in charge of the Leafs' 1989 NHL draft. He's the guy who made the final call, infamously using a trio of first-round picks to select three players—Thornton, Bancroft, and Rob Pearson—from the same team—the Belleville Bulls, who were coached and managed by Flynn. Stellick can't help but laugh either, confessing that bits and pieces of the folklore are all true in their own ways.

"Harold Ballard had a very lean front office, to say the least," he says.

STELLICK WAS PROMOTED to Leafs general manager a year and a half before he picked the three Bulls in April 1988 at the age of 30, becoming the youngest GM in NHL history. Before that, he'd filled in wherever he was asked in the smallest front office in the league. He was the mail boy. Then he was an executive assistant. Then he became the assistant to the general manager. Then assistant general manager. Throughout, he was the club's administrator and its travel agent.

"I did pretty well everything," Stellick said.

So by the time he was thrust into the GM job just a couple of months before the 1988 NHL Draft, Stellick had attended the league's eight previous drafts, sitting next to general manager Punch Imlach at his first two and general manager Gerry McNamara after that. He'd been there when the Leafs picked Bob McGill in 1980, Jim Benning in 1981 (though Benning, he recalls, wasn't in the building), the Ihnacak brothers in 1982, Russ Courtnall in 1983, Al Iafrate in 1984, Wendel Clark in 1985, Vincent Damphousse in 1986, and Luke Richardson in 1987.

When he took over, Stellick also had full confidence that his head scout, Floyd Smith, was a "really, really good head scout" in a thin scouting department because, a year earlier, Smith had argued hard for a kid out of the Swift Current Broncos by the name of Joe Sakic (who was taken 15th, later became a regular season and playoff MVP, and is now in the Hockey Hall of Fame) when the Leafs drafted Richardson seventh overall.

"That would have been a ballsy pick, a real ballsy pick, so I really respected Floyd Smith a lot," Stellick said of Smith's push to have McNamara nearly draft Sakic.

In the lead-up to his first draft as GM in 1988, with the Leafs set to pick sixth, Stellick tried to familiarize himself with the options available in the first round but left most of the rest up to his scouts. He knew that Mike Modano and Trevor Linden would go one-two, and that the draft really started with the Quebec Nordiques, who owned the third and fifth picks, which they used on defenceman Curtis Leschyshyn and right wing Daniel Dore. At fourth overall, with the pick between Quebec's, the Penguins selected Darrin Shannon, a left wing with the Windsor Spitfires on whom the Leafs had keyed in. With Shannon off the board, Stellick and his staff debated between physical Kingston Canadians left wing Scott Pearson (who they picked and went on to amass 615 penalty minutes and 98 points in 292 games) and Hull Olympiques star Martin Gelinas (who was picked immediately after by the Kings and went on to register 660 points across 1,273 games). Gelinas wasn't the only player the Leafs missed on with their Pearson selection, either. Three of the generation's best players were chosen after Pearson and Gelinas in quick succession, with one of the greatest American-born players in league history, Jeremy Roenick, going eighth out of Thayer Academy to the Blackhawks, future Selke Trophy winner and Hurricanes captain Rod Brind'Amour going ninth to the Blues, and the legendary Teemu Selanne going 10th to the Jets.

"At that point, we didn't scout them enough," Stellick conceded. "We weren't really looking, or able to look, at high schools and the American side, or Finland, like we should have been. That's where not having a deep scouting department hurt us. And John Brophy was the coach, and he wanted a more physical team and Scott seemed to bring that and the skill part with decent offensive stats."

In the second round, with the Leafs' 27th overall pick, Stellick took a flier on Peterborough Petes tough guy Tie

Domi, who wasn't ranked in the top three rounds by NHL Central Scouting.

"For a guy who was just a one-dimensional tough guy, his skating never ended up being the greatest, but he really improved his skating and he really improved his skill and more and more he really impressed us. We had traded our third-round pick to the Rangers so it was kind of all or nothing, and if you want the guy, you've got to get the guy. So Tie was who we targeted," Stellick said. "And his family was watching the draft and just after we took Tie the draft coverage ended, so his family got to see him get drafted by the Maple Leafs, which he always tells me when he sees me."

When it was over, the Leafs had selected six future NHL players in 1988, having also drafted goalie Peter Ing, a teammate of Shannon's; defencemen Ted Crowley and Len Esau; and centre David Sacco. With their last pick in the draft's 12th round, they also selected Peter DeBoer, a third player they liked from that Spitfires team, who never played an NHL game but went on to become a head coach in the league with the Panthers, Devils, Sharks, and Golden Knights.

"It's funny because we traded and got a guy named Paul Lawless from Vancouver and I made the trade with Pat Quinn and then he got back to me and said, 'The guy we like is Peter DeBoer,' so we traded Pete to Vancouver before he even became a Leaf," Stellick said. "And back then you couldn't get a hold of people because there were no cell phones, so I wasn't able to get in touch with him and then Floyd connected with him. So Pete kids with me that I drafted him and traded him and we never got to know each other."

THE LEAFS ARRIVED at the 1989 NHL draft in Bloomington, Minnesota, after a 10th consecutive season with a losing record (28–46–6), finishing last in the 10-team Campbell Conference and one point up on last in the league. Stellick arrived feeling more prepared than the first time around because he'd had a full season to oversee the operation, though they were still a bare-bones group. His Leafs held the third pick and had acquired the 12th and 21st selections (via the Flames) from the Flyers that March in exchange for goalie Ken Wregget at the trade deadline. Stellick knew it wasn't a strong draft and that the only way he was able to acquire two firsts for Wregget, who'd started the bulk of the Leafs' games over the previous three seasons, was because Flyers general manager Bobby Clarke likely felt the same way.

Heading in, the Leafs knew that the Nordiques, who held the first overall pick, were going to use it on Swedish sensation Mats Sundin, making him the first European player selected atop the NHL draft. Stellick's first target was WHL star Dave Chyzowski, who he'd made two trips to Kamloops to watch play and who went on to captain Canada to gold at the world juniors and win a Memorial Cup the next season before injuries derailed his promising career.

The night before the draft, Oilers general manager and head coach Glen Sather called Stellick in his hotel room to share info, wanting the Leafs to pick the best player at third overall so that the division rival Jets, who held the fourth overall pick, would lose out. After telling Sather he wanted Chyzowski, they eventually got to discussing backup plans, knowing there was a chance Chyzowski would be taken second by the Islanders.

If they didn't get Chyzowski, Stellick told Sather that they were debating between Thornton, a scrappy centre who'd just finished a 62-point, 59-game sophomore season in Belleville, and Stu Barnes, who'd just won the WHL's player of the year award with 141 points in 70 games with the Tri-City Americans.

"Hold on, I'll get our book here," Sather said, dropping the phone to look over the Oilers' draft list.

"We have Thornton ahead of Barnes," Sather added after picking the phone back up.

On draft day, when the Islanders picked Chyzowski and the Leafs' draft table debate continued as the clock counted down, Stellick's conversation with Sather was one of the things that tipped the scale toward Thornton. Then the Jets took Barnes, who played 16 years and 1,136 NHL games, posting 597 points.

In the Met Center, Thornton and Bancroft, who'd become fast friends in Belleville, sat next to each other in the crowd with their families and shared agent, Harry Francis. Thornton had no idea that the Leafs would pick him, let alone what would come next. He'd interviewed with several teams at his hotel in Bloomington, but the conversations were informal and none of Stellick, Floyd, Armstrong, or Woods ever tipped his hand.

While Thornton mingled with brass on the draft floor and conducted his round of media interviews, Bancroft and his family (who'd loaded up into a giant, fully loaded van to drive down to meet him at the draft after he'd flown in with Thornton and Francis) waited for his name to be called as the Leafs prepared to pick for a second time.

When they said "from the Belleville Bulls," his heart dropped.

When it wasn't his name who they called, announcing Pearson's instead, his heart sank further.

The Pearson pick was a peculiar one because he'd been limited to just 26 games in his draft year after breaking his scaphoid (a bone in his wrist). On top of that, while Thornton and Bancroft had been the Bulls' two top picks in the 1987 OHL draft, meaning they had two years of junior under their belts by the time draft day arrived, Pearson had stayed in Midget for a year longer. So his draft year was his rookie season, and his 26 games were his only sample of play.

Flynn, who watched it play out on TV from his place in Belleville, was a big backer of Pearson's (who posted 20 points in those 26 games as a rookie), though.

"I knew that Rob Pearson would be a really interesting pick, and I knew that scouts really liked his first 26 games, so it made sense that a team like Toronto that had an extra first could take a chance on him and still get a Scott Thornton early," Flynn said. "He showed lots of promise, both with his offensive instincts and his feistiness. And it was a different era at that time, but you could tell that he was going to be a hard-nosed, Rick Tocchet–type winger that could score. In those days, offensive wingers with jam were coveted players."

Thornton, too, remembers the fist pump he gave when Pearson was selected by the Leafs, because he'd developed a huge respect for his teammate in that single season.

"Rob Pearson was a hell of a hockey player," Thornton said.

Despite his more limited exposure, Pearson was actually the only one the Leafs had gone into the draft intent on targeting. When the Flyers went on a late-season tear and their pick kept falling in the draft as they rose in the standings, Stellick worried that Pearson wouldn't be available with their second pick.

"We really liked Rob Pearson a lot," Stellick said. "We were thrilled when we got Rob Pearson, we really were."

Bancroft, who had also drawn interest from the Hartford Whalers (who passed on him to select Bobby Holik with their first-round pick at 10th overall), came with some injury concerns of his own as well, having battled shoulder issues throughout his draft year.

As the Leafs' turn approached for a third time, Bancroft sat in the crowd awaiting his call while Stellick and his staff kicked around more names on the draft floor. Their primary target with the 21st overall selection was Kitchener Rangers right wing Steven Rice. But the New York Rangers snatched Rice a pick before theirs, taking him 20th overall.

"Ah, damnit," Stellick half-shouted, banging the palm of his hand on the table.

With Rice off the board, the Leafs' top-ranked forward was Cornell University commit Kent Manderville, and their top-ranked defencemen were Bancroft and another Cornell commit, Dan Ratushny. After briefly discussing the merits of taking Manderville, they decided they'd be better off taking a defenceman because they'd already drafted two forwards with their previous picks. Woods, who loved Bancroft, tipped the scales this time, completing the trifecta to take Bancroft, who'd posted 37 points in 66 games from Belleville's blue line, with the final pick of the first round.

The rest of the Leafs' 1989 draft has understandably been forgotten. Shortly after taking Bancroft, Stellick felt comfortable using some of his extra draft capital to try to upgrade his fledgling roster, dealing the team's second-round pick to the Flames (which they coincidentally used to select Manderville) in exchange for defenceman Rob Ramage, who'd play two productive seasons as an anchor of the Leafs' blue line (a trade Stellick remains proud of). With the team's fourth-round selection, he also chose University of Maine commit Matt Martin, who went on to play parts of four seasons as a depth defenceman with the Leafs.

But Stellick—and everyone else involved in that day—knows they're part of draft infamy and that the 1989 Leafs class will only be remembered for one thing.

At the time, it was a thrill for the three Bulls, who never imagined what did happen would happen. That night, the Thorntons, the Pearsons, and the Bancrofts gathered in one of their hotel rooms to celebrate.

"It was pretty shocking" Thornton said, "but it was a big deal to us."

The following season, the three of them got to attend their first NHL training camp together before they were each returned to Belleville for a final hurrah in the OHL, with Pearson scoring a team-high 48 goals in just 58 games, Thornton registering 49 points in 47 games, and Bancroft adding 43 points in 53 games from the blue line.

"It was exciting for us to go into our first training camp with some friends and someone to talk to and go to dinner with," Thornton said.

Fate, however, eventually pulled them in different directions.

In 1990, Thornton bounced between the Leafs, their AHL affiliate in Newmarket, and the Bulls in his first season of professional hockey. He spent his first six months with the team living out of a hotel in the back alley at Maple Leaf Gardens until he moved into Francis' apartment. The team, which was in the midst of another rebuild, cycled through two head coaches, with Doug Carpenter replacing Tom Watt late in the year and finishing 1–9–1 down the stretch. There were a lot of lonely nights in the press box and three meals a day sitting by himself in restaurants. Though he credits team-mates like Ramage, Brad Marsh, and Dave Hannan for their guidance, the odd invitation to their homes for dinner, and post-practice drills they'd run him through, Thornton found life as a 19-year-old in the NHL to be daunting.

"I wouldn't say it was a lot of fun my first year. It was really tough to try and figure things out. It was quite a different era in the sense that you're kind of left to fend for yourself. The whole time you're trying to figure out the professional side, which is, 'How do I play at this level?' and compete and become a man instantly," Thornton said. "It was a big struggle for me. It was a lot to handle."

After getting into just 33 games with the Leafs as a rookie, Thornton was then traded in his third training camp to Edmonton in a package that brought aging stars Grant Fuhr and Glenn Anderson to Toronto. Thronton went on to play 941 NHL games, picking up 285 points and 1,459 penalty minutes along the way, but his rocky start in Toronto followed him.

"I didn't really have time to mature and develop as a Leaf, and then it took me a few years to recover and bring myself back," he said.

Bancroft, who was born in Toronto but raised in Madoc, 30 minutes north of Belleville, never played a game for his childhood team. A little more than a year after the draft, Bancroft was dealt in November 1990 to the Bruins for Rob Cimetta, a 1988 first-round pick who went on to play parts of two seasons with the Leafs in his short-lived NHL career.

A couple of years after that, in 1993, he was part of another draft experience when the newly minted Florida Panthers took him in the expansion draft.

He was driving back home to Madoc from therapy in Peterborough when he stopped in at a friend's place and he was told the news. But his new opportunity with the Panthers didn't last long.

"When Florida picked me, according to Bobby Clarke, they were going to offer me a termination contact but they didn't know that my contract was up. So I went from getting picked, pretty excited, I'd had a decent year with more than 60 points playing in the IHL and the AHL, and then within a few days I found out that they weren't going to sign me. I went from being happy to being thrown to the side," Bancroft said.

Bancroft spent 16 years as a top defenceman in the AHL and IHL. He became a second bit of hockey trivia when his only two stints in the NHL came a decade apart (he played a lone game for the Blackhawks in October 1992 and five more with the San Jose Sharks in January 2002). In 1999, he won a Calder Cup with the Providence Bruins. In 2001, he led all AHL defencemen in points with 73 and was named to the league's first All-Star team. He retired in 2006 at the age of 36 with more than 1,000 professional games and nearly 2,000 penalty minutes.

Stellick's gamble on Pearson's limited experience actually ended up paying off when he was the only one of the three who stuck around in Toronto, playing three seasons for the Leafs before finishing his NHL career in Washington and St. Louis for another three years.

All these years later, Thornton and Bancroft remain like brothers. Bancroft was the best man at Thornton's wedding and the two still spend their summers (and winters) fishing and hunting together. Throughout their careers, Bancroft made frequent trips to Thornton's cottage on Crow Lake in Havelock, Ontario, a half hour west of Madoc, to train with his old friend.

In retirement, Thornton settled just outside of Collingwood, where he built his home, started a gym, briefly ran a CrossFit event company, and invested in a spa in the nearby Blue Mountain area called Scandinave, which remains a staple of the community and a destination for getaways in the province. He has raised his two kids in the area.

"I've dabbled a lot since I've retired. I don't sit around too much. I stay busy," Thornton said, laughing. "It's a really nice community up here."

When Bancroft retired, he moved back to Madoc and became a local real estate agent after having taken courses throughout his playing career. In doing so, he took up the family business from his father, Bob.

"My body told me that it was time to retire, then a week later I was selling homes. There was no lag time. I was ready to go. I knew that year was going to be my last and as a 36-year-old when you're not making millions of dollars, it's not worth it anymore to battle through it. I jumped right into this, and I haven't looked back in 15 years," Bancroft said.

From Madoc, Bancroft also got into coaching minor hockey, leading his son Dalton's 2001 age group's AAA team, the Quinte Red Devils. Ten of his players were drafted into the OHL and one, Zach Uens, went on to become an NHL draft pick of the Florida Panthers in the 2020 NHL Draft's fourth round.

In recent years, Bancroft has also done some public speaking. He always tries to stump people with his *two* bits of hockey trivia. He laughs about how in his new life in real estate in the Bellville area he gets more "Hey, you played for the Bulls" comments than Leafs recognition.

Thornton and Bancroft still keep in touch with Pearson from time to time, too. Thornton and Pearson got together to play golf one recent summer and picked up right where they left off. Bancroft bumped into Pearson frequently around Ontario's rinks when they both coached their sons and eventually when Pearson became the head coach and general manager of the Junior A Pickering Panthers, who often played Dalton's Trenton Golden Hawks.

"The hockey world's a small world," Bancroft said. "You don't know who you're going to run in to."

A few years back, Stellick also bumped into Thornton in the Blue Mountain village.

The first thing Thronton said was, "Man, the three Bulls thing gets brought up *all the time.*"

Each of Thornton, Bancroft, and Flynn still says there was nothing to it, and Stellick's version of events says so too.

"We had no clue," Bancroft said. "It's something that has never happened before and will likely never happen again."

Flynn, who was fired by the Bulls at the end of the 1989–90 season, went on to coach the OHL's Soo Greyhounds, Canadian university hockey's St. Francis Xavier University, the QMJHL's Moncton Wildcats and Saint John Sea Dogs, the NHL's Buffalo Sabres, and the WHL's Portland Winterhawks before landing with the Columbus Blue Jackets as an amateur scout in 2018. He, too, regularly bumps into Pearson and Bancroft at OJHL games and tournaments. And now that he's been on the other side of the sport as a scout, he can't believe an NHL team ever used three first-round picks on three players from the same team. One day, before a meeting with the Blue Jackets, he regaled the rest of the team's scouts with the story, and they couldn't believe it either.

"They were amazed that that could happen. I don't know if we're ever going to see that again in our lifetime," he said. "It was a remarkable story at that time, especially to have three kids go to a team two hours from Belleville and one of the most high-profile teams in the NHL. To have that happen again, boy, the stars would have to line up."

He doesn't think Stellick got them wrong, though. Scouting is much more wide-ranging today, he'll tell you, pointing to changes in the way teams background check players and conduct interviews, the combine's fitness testing, and the global reach of departments and the internet. He does think each would be first-round picks today regardless. "Those three kids, based off of the years they had and the skill level those players had, they were all legitimate first-round picks, no question about that," Flynn said. "So Toronto picked the right guys; it's just amazing that they ended up all being on the same team."

Stellick only ever ran the two drafts for the Leafs. He never got to oversee the development of the three Bulls as a result. In August 1989, a couple of months after the draft, he quit.

"I was not able to name my next head coach. Harold was like 87 and he would die eight months later and it was getting bad. I realized that something drastic had to happen and he was insistent that, God rest his soul, George Armstrong stay on as coach. And it was just different," Stellick said of the times. "It was tough to leave. You go through life without any regrets but that one has just always been tough. There was just a lot of stuff playing with a very unique owner in the office."

Rangers general manager Neil Smith had also done some, according to Stellick, "good old-fashioned tampering" while Stellick was still with the Leafs, quickly hiring him to become the assistant general manager in New York. After two seasons with the Rangers, Stellick returned to Toronto, where he become the a radio broadcaster with *The Fan 590* and later Sportsnet. In his absence, the team he'd helped build broke .500 in 1989–90, finishing 38–38–4 for sixth place in the Campbell Conference to return to the playoffs.

"I'm pleased that '89–90 team was still my team that I'd sculpted. It had all kinds of offence, it was tough. We had to work on defence, which hurt them a year or two later, but it was a lot of fun," Stellick said.

He knows the way the three Bulls picks look but says he didn't clue in until moments after they'd made their third pick.

"It kind of hit us at that point that, 'Jeez, we took three guys from the same team; that's kind of cool,'" Stellick said. "But we had not even thought about it."

The Bulls picks aren't the only ones of the 1989 draft that people give him a hard time about these days. After the Leafs took Thornton third, he knows he missed on another American when the Devils took future star and two-time Stanley Cup winner Bill Guerin fifth. Immediately after the Bancroft pick, the Nordiques also took Adam Foote, who became the defender Stellick was looking for with that pick and a captain of the Blue Jackets and Avalanche.

"People always say, 'You took Bancroft ahead of Adam Foote!?' and I always go, 'Bancroft wasn't even the best defencemen named Adam drafted at the time. Adam Bennett went earlier,'" Stellick said.

He still defends his picks.

"There have been some horseshit first-round picks after that by the Leafs. And really, Thornton had a decent NHL career and Rob Pearson, if he hadn't got hurt, I think he would have…" Stellick said, pausing as if not to get carried away. "Anyways…"

8

FROM A LOST DRAFT YEAR TO DEVELOPING THE LEAFS' LOST PROSPECTS

A S SOON AS Drake Berehowsky delivered the hit, searing pain shot through his body, and he knew that was something was seriously wrong. Instead of pushing through his opponent's chest to deliver the clean hit he was looking to hand out, he'd missed him—at top speed. When he did, he'd stuck out his right leg as a reflex, clipping his intended target with his knee and spinning off him. And now he was rolling on the ice in pain.

When the trainers finally got to him, all he could get out through that pain were the same few words, repeated until they picked him up and carried him down the tunnel to the dressing room.

"Get me off the ice as fast as you can!" he shouted. "Get me off the ice!"

As he laid in the room and they cut off his equipment, his mind raced and wandered as he talked himself into a panic.

My career is over, he thought to himself.

My dream is over.

My life is over.

Before that moment, before Berehowsky's knee popped and blew in the ninth game of his NHL draft year with the Kingston Frontenacs in the fall of 1989, he'd felt he was destined for stardom.

Everything about his hockey career to that point had gone exactly as it was supposed to.

BEREHOWSKY WAS BORN in January 1972 to immigrant parents, with a father from the United States and a mother who was born in Estonia. (His grandmother fled to Canada during the war and left his mother in Germany for a year before sending for her when she was just three years old.) He was raised in Etobicoke, close to where his dad was a schoolteacher at Western Technical-Commercial School in Toronto's West End. They settled there because his father didn't like to drive and never wanted to commute to his work. Ironically, though, when Berehowsky took up hockey as a way to fit in and to keep himself from going stir-crazy as a kid, almost all of the city's competitive hockey played out of its East End (which has reversed these days), forcing his dad into driving to all his games anyway.

Berehowsky quickly became one of the city's top players and a star defenceman of the Toronto Marlies' AAA team. He grew up going to Saturday 6 AM practices at Maple Leaf Gardens before the Leafs had their morning skates in advance of *Hockey Night in Canada*. One of his fondest childhood memories is of the Sunday morning he dragged his parents out of bed at 3 AM so they could take him down to the Gardens for 4:30 AM in the hopes that if he got there before his practice, he might be allowed to skate by himself before the rest of his teammates arrived. That morning, arena staff, who were still cleaning up from the Leafs game the night before, let him on the ice with three pucks and one light on, warning him that his shots better hit the net because Leafs owner Harold Ballard was sleeping in his apartment. (He still has the photo of him alone on the ice with one light on to prove it.)

By 15, he was already posting 46 points in 40 games with the Barrie Colts, who were then a Junior B team. At the end of that season, the OHL's Kingston Canadians (who became the Kingston Raiders and then the Kingston Frontenacs in quick succession in his first and second seasons with the team following a pair of ownership changes) selected him first overall in the 1988 OHL draft. In his rookie season in Kingston, he posted 46 points in 63 games, fourth among all the OHL's under-17 players. Before he injured himself early in his second season, Berehowsky, a 6'2", 200-plus pound defenceman who played a physical *and* talented game, had already posted 14 points in nine games on Kingston's backend. In the days before the injury, that impressive early play, which paced him to lead the league's defencemen in scoring that year, had brought swaths of NHL scouts through the Kingston Memorial Centre to watch him and pull him aside for post-game chats to express their interest.

Before he knew it, though, in the days after the injury, he'd moved from Kingston back to Toronto and was sitting in the office of Dr. Michael Clarfield, who was then the Leafs' head physician. In his first visit with Dr. Clarfield, when his muscles wouldn't relax to allow his knee to shift out during the tests the doctor ran, Berehowsky was misdiagnosed when Dr. Clarfield told him he didn't think it was anything serious. But when the pain, instability, and discomfort didn't fade and he returned to Dr. Clarfield for a second visit and a scope into his knee, the scope revealed a complete tear of his ACL and some structural issues with his right leg.

Hours later, Berehowsky, who'd never even heard of an ACL tear and knew nothing of the severity of knee injuries before then, woke up with a 20-pound cast on his leg to learn that following the scope, Dr. Darrell Ogilvie-Harris, another of the Leafs' old team physicians, had operated on him.

News of the surgery also came with news that his draft year was over. Both Ogilvie-Harris and Clarfield told him he would have to come to terms with setting his sights on next year's draft.

He remained in the cast for two and a half months, and a gruelling year of rehab followed.

To lift his spirits, his mom purchased some self-help books for Berehowsky to read. As a way of keeping himself motivated and out of the black hole he'd felt himself sink into, he read voraciously and did his own research into the knee problems that Detroit Red Wings captain Steve Yzerman had battled and overcome.

Beyond the reading, the only thing that kept Berehowsky going was the continued interest from NHL clubs in advance of the 1990 draft. Throughout the year, the Rangers, who would eventually hold the 13th overall pick, showed the most interest. David McNab, then an amateur scout for the Rangers (today he's the Ducks' longtime senior vice president of hockey operations), kept regular tabs on him, checking in to see how he was doing and even purchasing him tickets to several Leafs games so that he could at least watch some hockey during his time off.

Though there was no scouting combine at the time, several other teams also flew him into town to test out his knee themselves and take him to dinners or baseball games.

One of those final visits was with his hometown Maple Leafs, who held the 10th overall pick and were already familiar with his injury through their doctors. When his meetings with Leafs brass were over, they told him he was going to be their guy if he was still available, meaning McNab and the Rangers were never going to get the opportunity to select him.

In the final weeks ahead of the draft, which was set to be held for the first time in Vancouver, that information gave Berehowsky life.

The first thing he did was the first thing every kid did when they got that news: he got a haircut and he purchased a new suit. Then he and his family got on a plane and flew to Vancouver a week in advance of the draft to do some sightseeing.

On the day of the draft, though he knew the Leafs would take him if he got there, he didn't know if he'd go earlier, or if the Rangers would try to move up to grab him. While his eventual selection by the Leafs felt inevitable, he still had to wait anxiously in the stands for it.

And the blur that followed felt the same for him as it did for the other players—maybe even different because of all that he'd been through.

When they did call his name, it still felt surreal. So did everything that followed. The speech he made from the podium. Placing the hat on his head and lifting the jersey over his shoulders. The rush of interviews.

When it was over, he spent the night in a hotel room to which the Leafs invited all of the players and their families back to socialize, circling the room to meet scouts, the team's other picks (including future Leafs starting goalie Felix Potvin, whom the Leafs drafted 31st overall with their second-round pick that year), and other members of the organization he hadn't yet met through his rehab process or his pre-draft day with the team.

It didn't really sink in that he'd just become a first-round selection of his hometown team until he returned home to the unexpected chaos of it. When he arrived back to Toronto, the first thing he thought was *OK, I'm going to the cottage to wind down*, and so he quickly packed his bags to get away. But as he prepared to leave the house, his phone began to ring. When he picked up, there was a reporter on the other end of the line looking for an interview. Then came another. And another.

It wasn't until a few days later, when things had finally begun to settle down, that he managed to escape the city for a short while. When he returned, he spent the rest of the summer after his draft rehabbing his knee with Leafs athletic therapist Chris Broadhurst. Once he began to feel closer to 100 percent, he'd ride his bike down to Maple Leaf Gardens, where the security guys would open the side door and he'd ride right into the Leafs dressing room for treatment and skates. With each skate, he began to feel better and better about his ability to keep his career on the track it had been on before the injury.

Against the odds he'd even set for himself, Berehowsky made the Leafs out of camp the following fall as an 18-year-old, playing in eight games in October before a demotion back to Kingston and an eventual trade to the OHL's North Bay Centennials, where he finished the year.

In his second year post-draft, though, he was less successful in camp. The Leafs returned him to North Bay and he made just one appearance for the Leafs that year in January, playing the full season for the Centennials, where he posted a combined 113 points in 83 regular season and playoff games, winning CHL Defenseman of the Year. After losing in the 1992 OHL Final with the Centennials, Berehowsky joined the St. John's Maple Leafs and played in the final six games of their seven-game series against the Adirondack Red Wings in the Calder Cup Final, falling just short of a second championship that spring.

His knee and leg never did fully heal in those first couple of years after the draft. After being sent back to St. John's following his third training camp, a pin in his leg started to come out and he was forced to return to Toronto to have it removed. After a few weeks of additional rehab in Toronto, by the time Berehowsky returned to St. John's, a local municipal workers' strike, which had begun in December of that season, had raised tensions so high in the city that the team decided to forgo playing their home games and go on an extended road trip. Though the team briefly returned to St. John's in February to try to play home games again, unrest amongst the strikers spilled over when the team crossed over their picket lines to play. When they did, the protesters surrounded the team's bus and tried to tip it over while the players were on it, breaking several of its windows in the process. After the incident, the team, which had by then been joined by a healthy Berehowsky, went back on the road for a second time, playing all its games away from Memorial Stadium until its second-round playoff series that April against the Cape Breton Oilers. The season was one of the most tumultuous in the history of the Leafs' first AHL stay in St. John's, with ownership threatening to relocate the team to Charlottetown, Prince Edward Island. The team eventually took over the Halifax Metro Centre for its first-round playoff home games. By the time St. John's returned to Newfoundland to play Cape Breton on April 29 of that year, it had been four full months—and 44 games on the road—away from its home rink, with so-called home games played wherever it could find an available arena (in Stephenville, Newfoundland, for two games after the bus incident, and then in Toronto, Montreal, Cornwall, Charlottetown, and Halifax).

Through it all, though, Berehowsky calls that season, his first full professional one, the most memorable of his career. With St. John's as a 20-year-old, he became one of the league's best defenders almost right away, posting 27 points in 28 games. That year, he also played a further 41 games in the

NHL, posting 19 points on a Maple Leafs team that went all the way to its infamous defeat to Wayne Gretzky's Los Angeles Kings in Game 7 of the conference finals. He didn't play in any of those playoff games, though, and split his time between the Leafs' NHL and AHL clubs one last time again the next year, playing another 49 games for Toronto in 1993–94. A 22-year-old Berehowsky eventually stuck in the NHL full-time in 1994–95 with the Leafs, only to be dealt to the Penguins at that year's deadline for defenceman Grant Jennings. Though he never had the career he felt he was destined for before the injury, or the one the Leafs gambled on when they drafted him 10th overall, Berehowsky went on to play 571 NHL regular season and playoff games for six NHL organizations, registering 153 points and nearly 900 penalty minutes. After additional stops in Edmonton, Nashville, Vancouver, and Phoenix, he finished his NHL career with a nine-game stint with the Leafs at the end of the 2003–04 season after the team reacquired him from a second stint with the Penguins in a trade for defenceman Richard Jackman.

BEREHOWSKY ALWAYS SAID that if hockey didn't work out, he would have followed in his father's footsteps to become a teacher. So once he'd retired from his playing days following two years in Europe prompted by the 2004–05 NHL lockout, Berehowsky turned his attention to coaching and found a gig as an assistant coach with the OHL's Barrie Colts in 2007 at the age of 35. After two seasons in Barrie, he made the jump to the professional ranks, joining the AHL's Peoria Rivermen as an assistant coach. After Peoria, he then pounced at his first head coaching job with the ECHL's Orlando Solar Bears in 2012, followed by two seasons as the head coach of the WHL's Lethbridge Hurricanes, two more as an associate head coach with the OHL's Sudbury Wolves, and a return to Orlando to take over behind the Solar Bears bench for a second time in 2016—a role that also came with the team's general manager duties, which he still holds today.

When he took the Solar Bears job for a second time, it also marked his third time as a member of the Leafs organization, who held Orlando as their ECHL affiliate for five seasons from 2013 through 2018. (The Leafs only ended the affiliation because they eventually reached an agreement with the ECHL's expansion Newfoundland Growlers to return professional hockey to St. John's.) Faced with a decision on whether to keep himself and his young family in Orlando or move into a different role within the Leafs organization, Berehowsky decided to stick with the Solar Bears as the NHL's Lightning took over the affiliation for the 2018–19 season.

In retirement from his playing days, Berehowsky and his partner, Danielle, also started Statstrack, a hockey analytics firm and software company that enables teams to track their own data, cut their own tape, and produce live intelligence reports (reports that Berehowksy and clients in the CHL, USHL, college hockey, the DEL, and the CJHL use in their work with players).

In his second career as a coach, Berehowsky has gone from prospect to teacher in his own way after all. Two and a half decades after the Leafs made him one of their draft picks, he was overseeing the development of theirs, helping former Leafs prospects Mason Marchment, Kasimir Kaskisuo,

J.J. Piccinich, Martins Dzierkals, Garret Sparks, and Aaron Luchuk at some point along their journey with the Solar Bears—or would-be Leafs prospects Andrew Nielsen and Giorgio Estephan along theirs in Lethbridge.

Today, when he looks back on his life in hockey as a player and the painful draft year that led him to the Leafs back in 1990, he considers himself only fortunate for how it all turned out. He's too far removed from how he felt at the time, when the disappointment of the injury felt like it had crushed him.

"At that age, you think you're invincible. It was a shock to my system. It was a long year. It was a long rehab. I was very fortunate to even be able to get drafted given how bad it was. I consider myself so lucky that the Leafs drafted me after only playing nine games," he said.

When he talks about that rehab process, he pauses to marvel at how ahead of his time Broadhurst was, too.

"He knew that these injuries weren't the end of the world and he put a plan in place to get me to where I wanted to be," Berehowsky said of the Leafs' former head athletic therapist, who now runs Toronto's Sport Medicine Clinic.

Berehowsky also credits his mom for keeping him focused on what mattered most, for instilling in him an attitude that said, "No matter what you do, do it the best that you can," and for keeping him reading and learning so that he wouldn't lose sight of his dream.

When he looks back on his draft day, he still can't wrap his head around the experience of getting selected, after all that he'd been through, by *his* team. There aren't many, he says, who get to go from practicing on the Maple Leaf Gardens ice as a kid to paying on it as a *Maple Leaf.*

"It was pretty amazing. You're waiting there and then your name finally gets called and for me especially, because I sat out a year, I felt so privileged," he said.

He laughs as he retells his post-draft cottage story and the delay he had to put on his trip up north as those phone calls started to roll into his family's home.

"I didn't realize what a big deal it was," he said. "I don't think anybody fully realizes the coverage that Toronto players get."

He says he never really felt the pressures of being a 10th overall pick, though. He was having too much fun. He remembers too fondly the sold-out buildings of that Calder Cup Final run when he first arrived in St. John's, or the NHL buildings full of Leafs jerseys when they travelled to places like Edmonton and Florida, or that year on the road during the strike, to have any regrets about how any of the rest of it turned out for him.

"I wanted to be up with the big club and play with them, but we had such a good time down in St. John's," Berehowsky said. "It was just such an amazing thing to be a part of the Toronto Maple Leafs that you were just happy. And wherever I was, they treated us well. I was pretty fortunate, all told."

And he's thankful that the Leafs believed in him enough a second time to trade for him and a third to trust him to run their ECHL team all those years later.

His second career in the sport has also given him a greater appreciation for how his first one played out. In it, he got to watch kids who look just like he did try to do what he was so lucky to do for parts of 12 NHL seasons.

"There's nothing better than being a hockey player, but the one thing I've come to learn is that there's a lot more pressure on players nowadays. There are a lot more camps. There's social media, which I promise you they read. So they see where they stand on the ice constantly and then they have this constant wave of information, as well," Berehowsky finished. "When I played, I had no idea what was going on and I never came from a hockey family, so I didn't understand any of it. And maybe that was a good thing because I didn't feel any type of pressure. Kids now train 12 months a year, where we took six weeks off in the summer. They play all of this spring hockey, too. It's amazing how different it is. It's a 12-month game now."

But he loves nothing more than being a part of that process and shaping the direction of today's players in some small way. Right through to the end of his time with the Solar Bears, he still pinched himself every time he stepped behind the Solar Bears bench.

"I've always wanted to stay involved in hockey. I think it's the coolest game and I think I'm so lucky and fortunate to live my dream and I've always wanted to teach people what I've been taught," Berehowsky said. "I've had so many great coaches that have taught me so much and so many great players I've played with that I've learned things from, so I've always wanted to give back to the game. It's an amazing sport."

9

A BLOCKBUSTER TRADE'S FORGOTTEN PIECE

T **HE HISTORY OF** the NHL draft isn't limited to the names that are called—there are also the trades that take place on its arena floors. Draft day has always been a natural place for transactions, as teams come together in the aftermath of playoff triumph or defeat to prepare for free agency and look ahead. General managers in the salary cap era wax poetic about how much easier it is to make a deal at the draft, when everyone feels like they've got money to spare and the flexibility to make something happen, than it is to pull one off at the actual trade deadline.

The Leafs' history at the draft is no different. Some of their most notable recent trades have, for better or worse, happened on draft weekend—the Tyler Biggs move-up, the

Luke Schenn–for–James van Riemsdyk swap, the Frederik Andersen trade. Others have happened on July 1 at the opening of free agency following conversations that began a week earlier at the draft—the Phil Kessel trade, the Nazem Kadri trade.

But there has never been a bigger transaction in Leafs history—and few bigger in the draft—than the one that took place on June 28, 1994.

When Gary Bettman stepped to the podium at the Hartford Civic Center to make it official, the crowd fell silent.

"I'd like to announce the following trade between Quebec and Toronto," he said.

When he began reading off the names and picks involved, the crowd audibly gasped twice, first when he said Mats Sundin's name and then again when he said Wendel Clark's, the noise crescendoing into a murmur that extended over the stadium and reverberated through the broadcast.

The Nordiques had made Sundin the first overall pick in the 1989 draft just five years earlier, and the 23-year-old had already racked up 334 points in 324 games across four seasons in Quebec, including a 114-point campaign as the league's 11th-leading scorer in 1993. Clark had just captained the Leafs to two deep playoff runs, was already one of the team's most beloved players ever, and was fresh off scoring a career-high 46 goals in just 64 games. (Had he maintained that rate across 82 games, his 59-goal pace would have challenged Pavel Bure, who scored 60 in 76, for the Rocket Richard Trophy, besting Brett Hull's 57 in 81 for second most.)

"I had a feeling there'd be a trade. I've had that feeling every year for the last five years now the way it's been around here. I'm not shocked but I'll miss Toronto," a visibly angry Clark told reporters later that day.

The rest of each of their stories has been told and written. The Leafs traded their 14th captain for their 16th when Sundin was eventually named Doug Gilmour's replacement in 1997, in what was by then his fourth of 13 seasons with the organization. Clark played just one season as an assistant captain with the Nordiques before the fledgling franchise moved to Denver. Less than two seasons after the trade, he was back in Toronto wearing an "A" underneath Gilmour for one season and then Sundin for his first. Sundin never carried the Leafs as far as the Cup, but he twice led them to the conference finals in 1999 and 2002 and the trade survived as a home run that brought an Olympic gold medalist, eight-time All-Star, and future Hall of Famer to Toronto.

But there were also six other pieces involved in the transaction whose lives and careers were impacted by that moment—and a web of others who were dealt and redealt to acquire them. Defenceman Sylvain Lefebvre's move from Toronto to Quebec as a small part of the deal led him to three years as an assistant captain with the Avalanche after the Nordiques moved—winning a Stanley Cup with them in 1996—and eventually a job as a scout and assistant coach with the Avalanche, which has led to a near-two-decade-long career behind NHL and AHL benches. Prospect Landon Wilson, who the Leafs had drafted 19th overall a year earlier, never got a real look with the Avalanche after he was a part of the deal. He was traded a couple of years later to the Bruins as part of a subsequent move that brought back another 19th overall pick (which they used on a different defenceman and longtime NHLer Robyn Regehr). Those two early trades preceded a career of bouncing from one NHL club—and its AHL affiliate—to another for Wilson. Veteran defenceman Garth Butcher's move from the Nordiques to the Leafs led to his retirement when his lone season in Toronto became the last of his career. The teams also swapped 1994 first-round picks, with Toronto moving up from 22nd to 10th as part of the trade. The Leafs turned around and dealt the 10th overall pick (which became AHL-NHL journeyman Nolan Baumgartner) and Rob Pearson to Washington for veteran Mike Ridley, who'd just posted 70 points in 81 games as the Capitals' leading scorer, and the 16th overall pick, which they used on goalie Eric Fichaud. Fichaud, who went on to play in an NHL net 95 times, never played any of those games for the Leafs after he was dealt again in April 1995 for forward Benoit Hogue, a 1995 third-round pick (which became Ryan Pepperall, who never made it past the farm team in St. John's) and a 1996 fifth-round pick (which became fighter Brandon Sugden, whose minor pro career ended due to ugly post-concussion syndrome realities he has spoken openly about). The Nordiques used the 22nd overall pick on Jeff Kealty, who played just one pro season in the IHL after he graduated from Boston University but has worked as a scout, director of scouting, and assistant general manager with the Nashville Predators for more than 20 years.

But none of the trade's forgotten-about pieces were impacted by it quite like 20-year-old Todd Warriner.

TODD WARRINER WATCHED the 1994 NHL draft from his grandfather Art's house in Blenheim, Ontario. He was there with his parents, Ivan and Janet, and his sister, Julianna, because they lived in the Chatham-Kent countryside outside of the small town of a few thousand people and Art was the only one who had TSN. There was already discussion about a potential trade between his Nordiques and the Leafs as the broadcast went live.

Once Bettman stepped to the podium, Warriner and his dad turned to each other, exchanging a hopeful glance that he may be involved in the trade that was to come.

"Well, maybe this is it," they said to each other.

They were hopeful for myriad reasons that spanned all the way back to his own draft two years earlier.

In advance of the 1992 NHL draft in Montreal, Warriner was one of its star prospects. That year, he'd scored 41 goals and 83 points in 50 games, which made him a second-team All-Star in the CHL and won him the CHL Top Draft Prospect Award as the league's No. 1–ranked draft-eligible player.

In advance of the draft weekend, Lightning president and general manager Phil Esposito, who held the first overall pick, had flown Warriner into Tampa and called him once a week to deliver the same message: "You're my guy, you're my guy," he'd told him.

On the Thursday before the draft, Warriner's agent, Don Meehan, picked him up in his convertible and drove him to Montreal, stopping at Harry Rosen along the way to buy him his "first overall suit." But that Friday, the mood dampened when Meehan received a phone call in his hotel room from Esposito explaining a change of plans. In their first year as an expansion team, Tampa's Esposito told Meehan he wanted to let his scouts run the table and his scouts had decided in their final meeting that they preferred Czech defenceman Roman Hamrlik.

After hanging up the phone, Meehan quickly called Warriner, who answered from his hotel room as he prepared to leave for dinner, less than 24 hours before he was supposed to head to the arena to rise to its podium. When Meehan was done relaying Esposito's message, Warriner spoke out in disbelief.

"Well, shit, what happens now then?" he said.

"Well, I think we might be able to get you to Toronto at No. 8," Meehan answered.

"Fuck, eight? I'm going to fall to eight? Oh, my god. That's going to be a bit of a story. Am I all of a sudden the eighth best player?" he replied.

The news was particularly shocking because Warriner had had discussions with a few teams throughout the season and into April, but he hadn't interviewed with any team other than Tampa in the six weeks leading up to the draft.

"Not one team," Warriner said on a phone call from his Southern Ontario home in the summer of 2021, nearly three decades later. "Everybody just sort of assumed that I was going to Tampa and there was no reason to talk to Warriner."

Though he didn't come right out and tell his family that he expected to go first overall, he *did* tell them that he had a good feeling, so many of them who joined him on the draft floor were expecting him to get drafted right away—and there wasn't enough time for him to warn them.

Due to how late in the process they learned that Esposito wasn't going to be able to pick him, Warriner and Meehan sat in their seats completely blind to where he was going to go. "We had literally no idea," he said.

After the Lightning started things off by taking Hamrlik, the Senators selected Alexei Yashin and the Sharks followed suit with defenceman Mike Rathje.

Then came the Nordiques, who were the only team Meehan didn't want to select Warriner. He shared the hockey world's concerns about their ownership and a weakening Canadian dollar. (The early 1990s were an era of significant financial turmoil for the Nordiques, Flames, Senators, and Oilers as salaries rose with the U.S. dollar, resulting in a Senators ownership change and the Nordiques' move, and nearly a move by the Oilers and Flames, as well.)

With Warriner's family to his left and Meehan to his right, longtime NHL scout and general manager Pierre Gauthier, who then worked as a scout for the Nordiques, made eye contact with Meehan, their jersey tucked under his arm, to mouth, "We're taking your guy."

"Oh, shit, Quebec's going to take you," Meehan told Warriner with a nudge.

At the time, Warriner didn't really care, not fully understanding the machination that Meehan had to consider. Warriner doesn't remember much of what happened in the moments after they called his name and he descended the stadium's steps to meet them on the floor, either. There was a blur of interviews, which he guesses he spun his wheels through. There was glad-handing. But his first vivid memory of the moments after the pick is of the cheer he got from its French Canadian crowd as he pulled on the Nordiques jersey. In the moment, he found the crowd standing to cheer him to be a bit much. The reception, he said, was incredible. And then it dawned on him that the reason they were so supportive was because Eric Lindros *hadn't* done it a year earlier when the Nordiques had selected him first overall.

That was really the only nice moment he had with the Nordiques organization, though. In his first year as a member of the organization, he and Meehan quickly learned that he wasn't going to get comparable money to the players who were selected around him. After completing his OHL career with the Spitfires and the Kitchener Rangers following a trade, he spent his second postdraft season training out of Calgary and travelling the world with Team Canada in advance of the 1994 Winter Olympics in Lillehammer, Norway. He played in 54 games for Canada that year, participating in the Deutschland Cup as well as exhibitions against NHL teams and tours of Europe in search of new opponents on a team that rotated a slew of players in and out and eventually included Paul Kariya and Czech defector Petr Nedved (once he became a Canadian citizen).

The Leafs, who would have indeed taken him eighth overall more than a year earlier had he been available when they selected center Brandon Convery (who went on to play 50 of his 72 career NHL games for the Leafs in parts of two seasons), kept a close eye on Warriner, watching him in a game at Maple Leaf Gardens in January against the Americans before following him to Lillehammer in February.

Leafs general manager Cliff Fletcher then sought out Warriner's parents in the crowd during one of Canada's warmups.

"Hey, I'm Cliff Fletcher," he told them from the row behind them inside Lillehammer's Håkons Hall.

"Yeah, we know who you are," Janet answered.

"I just wanted to say hello and say that we're really fond of your son and we'd like to try to get him in a deal at some point," Fletcher told them.

Armed with that information, Janet and Ivan decided not to tell their son until after the Olympics were finished, believing it was best not to distract him with it. It wasn't until after the tournament was over, when Canada had returned with a silver medal after falling to the Swedes in a dramatic shootout (a gold medal game that included Peter Forsberg's now-famous, postage-stamped one-handed goal) and Warriner had returned with an ankle injury, that his dad tried to soften the blow with details of their run-in with Fletcher.

After the Olympics, Warriner and his bum ankle joined the Nordiques for his first official professional stint with its AHL team, the Cornwall Aces, and he played in 10 of their playoff games. But when the year was done and uncertainty loomed over the Nordiques and his place within them, he wondered if anything would come of Fletcher's February words. The interest the Leafs expressed to Meehan and then Warriner's parents wasn't his only connection to the team to that point, either. A couple of years before his own draft, Warriner had visited longtime Leafs athletic therapist Chris Broadhurst and the team's doctors to rehab a knee injury.

"I'd spent a fair bit of time around the staff. I knew everybody," Warriner said.

Though he didn't know many of their players, he'd also gotten to know Clark through his Windsor head coach Brad "Motor City Smitty" Smith, who'd played on the Leafs in the '80s, and Meehan, who also represented him.

"I knew him from Madison Avenue summers," Warriner joked of time spent at Toronto's Madison Avenue pub with the Leafs legend.

While he was thrilled by his inclusion in the trade when Bettman delivered the details, he actually caught himself feeling a little disappointed that Clark, who was also one of his favourite players, was going the other way.

The move was also a personal thrill, as a kid from Ontario, and a much-needed professional change of scenery. Once he arrived back home to his parents' place after the draft, there was already a message from Meehan, who was on good working terms with the Leafs' brass, sharing in his excitement.

"Quebec was going sideways, and just trying to get a contract was a struggle there. We couldn't even get into the plans there," Warriner said.

Because the move happened before his off-season had really begun, it also made for a fun summer. In the days after the trade, Fletcher brought Warriner to Toronto to meet everyone and promise him an opportunity. He spent part of that summer training in Toronto under Leafs assistant coach Mike Kitchen, who would regularly bring a bunch of the local players out to Christie Pits, an urban park in the city's West End, to go for runs led by Doug Gilmour and himself. After their runs, they'd usually end up at Madison Avenue or the

Brunswick House, another popular Toronto bar the players frequented.

"I was just a pretty wide-eyed kid at the time," he said, laughing at the memories of getting dragged around town by Gilmour and his crew.

In his first training camp with the team, though, things went about as poorly as they could have. He was hit in the face with a puck in just his second scrimmage. His eye closed over, and the Leafs wouldn't let him skate for a few days until he could open it again. Two practices after he got back, he crashed into the boards and dislocated his shoulder. And then, just as camp broke, the league entered a lockout.

With his arm in a harness, the Leafs sent him to St. John's to join the farm team, where things got worse when he tried to play when he wasn't fully healthy in an effort to make an impression. In the process, he fell out of favour with St. John's head coach Tom Watt, who had him bouncing in and out of the lineup until Christmas.

"I wasn't really part of Tom Watt's plan and I kept thinking, 'This guy isn't going to play me and I'm not healthy enough to get more ice time anyways, so I don't have a leg to stand on,'" Warriner said.

By the time the lockout ended in January, his start in St. John's had gone so poorly that he was shocked when the Leafs called him up for his NHL debut and a two-week stint with the big club. The call-up didn't help him get back on track, though. After one back-to-back against the Red Wings, he left the two games thinking, *Holy cow, this is the NHL?* And, *Wow, I need to get a whole lot better.*

"I was nowhere near ready. I'd been hurt, I hadn't played enough, and when you're living in Newfoundland and you're not playing, you're only doing one thing," Warriner said, chuckling to himself about the bad habits that carried over from Madison Avenue and the Brunswick House. "I had to take stock of where I was at, to be completely honest."

The following summer, the then 21-year-old's perspective—and work ethic—changed. He moved into one of Meehan's apartments in Toronto, and he got to work rehabbing his "still messed up" ankle and shoulder a few times a week for three months.

The results followed when he played well in his second training camp, a run of play that left him thinking, *Wow, I should be close* when he was asked to join the team's final 28 players in Collingwood to finish out the preseason. As the camp's end neared, he was then invited into a meeting with head coach Pat Burns and Kitchen.

"Well, you've had a pretty good run…" Burns told him.

Well, that doesn't sound like my run's coming to an end, he thought to himself.

"…but we're going to send you down. And I don't know what happened last year, but you have to earn your promotion."

Warriner pleaded his case.

"I think I can play, and I don't want to go to the minors because I'm not sure Tom Watt likes me and I don't think he's going to play me. He wouldn't play me last year in the playoffs and I don't know how that's going to change," Warriner told them.

"The game doesn't owe you anything," Burns told him, fully closing the door on an immediate opportunity.

Determined to prove them—and Watt—wrong, things went better the second time around, and a month into the season Warriner earned a promotion when forward Bill Berg went down with an injury.

That second call-up changed the trajectory of his career, and though he never became the player he or the Nordiques thought he would, Warriner spent the next seven seasons in the NHL before he was ever sent back to the AHL, five of which were spent with the Leafs. On February 20, 1999, he became a small part of Leafs history when he scored the first ever goal at the newly opened Air Canada Centre. After stops in Tampa Bay, Phoenix, Vancouver, Philadelphia, and Nashville, he finished his NHL career with 154 points in 453 games, including 253 with the Leafs.

Fletcher stood by him every step of the way, trading for him three different times in his career (first with the Leafs, then the Lightning, then the Coyotes). Whenever he sees Fletcher, Warriner thanks him for believing in him.

"I always say you need a guy in your corner and for me that guy was Cliff Fletcher. I might not have had an NHL career if not for Cliff," Warriner said. "He went to bat for me, and you need that."

He eventually left the NHL behind in 2003 and spent six more seasons playing professionally in Finland, Switzerland, and Germany before retiring in 2009.

When he looks back at his two draft day experiences in 1992 and 1994, he's now able to laugh about both. Whenever he now watches the draft, he sees his own naivety in the kids who are picked and Meehan's gears turning in the agents seated next to them.

"I didn't really care that the Nordiques drafted me because I didn't really know any of the political backroom stuff," Warriner said. "That changes as your career moves along."

In retirement, he took up coaching with the University of Windsor's men's hockey team and broadcasting in junior hockey, first for Spitfires games and then as part of Sportsnet's CHL coverage.

Both roles gave him new perspective of his own draft experience, his development from prospect to player, and the way the game has changed.

"It's even more competitive now, the depth of talented players. Even the ones we get at the University of Windsor, I think about how there are players in our loop who I coach now or against who I'd loved to have had as a linemate in the minors because they're that good. It really came full circle when I went to Europe later in my career, too, and I went, 'Whoa, that guy's good, who's that?'" Warriner said. "For every Russian that comes over, there's a couple that don't that could come over and play but they're making $2 million in the KHL. Some of the German players between Leon Draisaitl and Uwe Krupp, there were some darn good players who could've played. And the same was true of the Swiss and Finns. Even some of the players I played with, I'd go, 'Try it' and two of three would always go, 'Yeah, I'd like to, but I can just play here and make $150,000 at home and I don't want to get stuck in the minors in a place I don't want to be.'"

These days, he says hockey fans are more likely to recognize him for his broadcasting work with Sportsnet than as a former Leaf.

His years with the Leafs remain the fondest of his career, though.

He enjoyed St. John's a little *too* much in those early years, which he'll be the first to admit.

"Newfoundland was incredible. I remember thinking, 'This is a bad place for the minor league team because the guys love it here.' I used to always say that you want the minor league spot to be OK, but you don't want it to be that good because you need there to be an incentive to get out of there. There was a point late in that first year where [journeyman forward] Kelly Fairchild and I were both hurt and the team went on the road for 12 days and we didn't go, so you're just on the island left to your own devices and having a little too much fun and then I remember midway through it we looked at each other and we were like, 'We've got to get it together here a little bit. This isn't what we're supposed to be doing,'" he said, laughing to himself. "And that's really the truth. I liked the lifestyle, and the guys had a lot of fun out there. It was a great place to live, and it feels like it's a long way from the NHL."

Were it not for the Sundin–Clark trade, the shoulder injury, or the reality check that was his five-game stint with the Leafs in that first year, Warriner's not sure if he ever would have made it.

"There's a critical point where you have to take stock and figure it out or not. I realized I wasn't putting the work in that I needed to yet. I was 20 and I needed to get my shit together," Warriner said. "Otherwise, like so many guys who played in Newfoundland, I'd still be there."

Though he and Sundin only knew each other through his two training camps with the Nordiques before the trade, that small familiarity brought them closer together when they both arrived in Toronto not really knowing any of the other players. Today, whenever they run into each other at events in Toronto, they light up. During a recent round of golf, Warriner and one of his old teammates, Matt Martin, called Sundin from the course to share some laughs and memories.

"I love Mats. We were instantly connected thanks to the trade. We spent a lot of time together in Toronto at dinners in the city. He lived south of Bloor on Bay for quite some time, and a bunch of us who lived downtown would spend the afternoons at his place. He was awesome. He was good to us," Warriner said. "And the older guys, too. When we first got there, the Dave Andreychuks and the [Doug] Gilmours and the Dave Elletts took care of us. And just before I left, Mats was the leader and the guy who was bringing people in. We have a good friendship. We were tight."

10

THE LATEST PICK

THE NHL DRAFT'S various iterations have produced different lengths over the years. The shortest draft in NHL history was its third in 1965, a draft considered so weak on talent that the Leafs decided they weren't even going to participate and just 11 picks were made in total, of which only two played NHL games. It peaked three and a half decades later, when the NHL's 2000 expansion ballooned the league's size to 30 teams at a time when the draft was already nine rounds long. So for five years before the draft downsized to its current seven-round format in 2005, an average of 291 players were selected each June.

The Leafs made their two latest draft selections in team history during that stretch, coincidentally picking 285th overall *twice*. One of those picks, Pierce Norton, was selected in 2004 out of Thayer Academy, a prep school in Braintree, Massachusetts. He played four seasons at Providence College but failed to stick with two ECHL teams, playing a combined

13 games for the Wheeling Nailers and Alaska Aces and never appearing at Leafs camp. The other, Staffan Kronwall, was selected six picks before the end of the 2002 NHL draft a few months before his 20th birthday, overcame tragedy as a child, carved out a brief NHL career in the shadow of his big brother, became a staple of the Swedish national team, and helped the KHL's Lokomotiv Yaroslavl rebuild in the aftermath of a tragedy of their own.

KRONWALL WAS BORN in Jarfalla, a suburb a little more than 20 minutes outside of Stockholm, which today is home to 80,000 people, on September 10, 1982. He was raised as the youngest of three boys in a hockey family, with all three playing defence. His dad, Hans, was the local team manager for the 1977-born age group of the Jarfalla Hockey Club, for which his oldest brother, Mattias, played. Niklas, the family's middle son who is a year and a half older than Staffan, became a star at an early age. When the three boys weren't playing organized hockey, they spent all their spare time each winter at the local soccer field near their home, which was flooded and turned into an outdoor rink.

At an early age, though, Staffan and the Kronwalls' lives changed. On Niklas' 11th birthday, Hans didn't wake up, passing of a heart attack in his sleep. Hans' death ruined the nine-year-old Staffan and left the family's matriarch, Tove, as the single mother of three growing boys. In the years that followed, because Tove worked a full-time job for copy machine maker Xerox to support the boys and keep them in hockey, Staffan had to grow up quickly, learning at a very young age to lead an independent life. As each of them grew older and made the jump up levels, joining the second-tier Huddinge IK and then the top-tier Djuragardens IF programs, both of which were located on the other side of the city, they also learned to get themselves to and from games and practices, with Tove usually alternating to pick up one of the three boys from school for hockey, leaving the other two siblings to return home, cook their own meals, and make the hour-and-a-half-long train and bus ride across the city to play by themselves. As Staffan made his way up the ranks, he got into the habit of doing his schoolwork on the nightly transit trips back from the rink, usually not arriving home until 10 PM.

"It was a tough time in our lives. We grew up early. We had to take responsibility. I'm sure Mom wasn't happy with us travelling across the city at that young age but that was the drive we had. There was no way she could stop us. And she was very involved, she came when she could, but she couldn't pick up three kids at the same time," Staffan said. "We had to learn to group up ourselves."

In the years after Hans' sudden death, Niklas began to build a reputation as one of the best young hockey players in Sweden, trademarking early the open-ice hits that would later become a hallmark of his 15-year career with the Red Wings (a career that included eight seasons as Detroit's assistant captain, an Olympic gold with Sweden in 2006, an Olympic captaincy in 2014, a world championships gold and MVP nod, and a 2008 Stanley Cup that made him a member of hockey's illustrious Triple Gold Club). Things didn't come quite as easily for Staffan and Mattias, though. When Niklas was made a first-round pick of the Red Wings in the 2000

NHL draft, Staffan, then 17, didn't think he had any NHL prospects of his own.

The following season, when he entered what should have been his NHL draft year in 2000–01, neither he nor his agent made any attempt to get him selected or enter him into the draft. Though he played for the local state team and made his pro debut with Huddinge IK in Sweden's low-level pro league, he went undrafted and had to that point never represented Sweden internationally.

A year after that, in 2001–02, Staffan played his first full season of pro hockey as a 19-year-old. He was also named to Sweden's national team for the first time, representing his country at the 2002 World Juniors, held that year in Pardubice and Hradec Kralove, Czech Republic.

"It was very different for me and my brother because Nik was already a huge talent at a very young age. For me, I was a big body, and it took a lot of time for me to grow into it. I was pretty late in my development. It wasn't until I was 18 years old basically where I really took a big step," Staffan said.

Again, though, when the draft came, he didn't expect to get picked or pay it any attention.

"Every kid growing up has a dream of playing in the NHL, but I didn't think it was a reality. I thought it was too far away. Even when I made the world juniors, it was a huge stage but I never thought about it as a draft stage. I thought it was an honour to represent my country. And then a lot of things began to happen for me in that year," Staffan said.

The 2002 draft, which was actually held in Toronto for just the second time at the then new Air Canada Centre, took place on June 22 and 23. Staffan didn't learn that he'd been picked in its ninth round until June 24, a day after it was all over, when he got a phone call from Stockholm-based Leafs amateur scout Thommie Bergman.

"Hey, welcome to the team," Bergman told Staffan.

"Oh wow, OK, I didn't even know but thank you," Staffan answered.

Bergman chuckled, telling Staffan they actually would have drafted him a year earlier had he opted in. Staffan laughed back, explaining to Bergman that he didn't even know how it worked.

And that was it. Bergman told Staffan he wanted to send him a Leafs hat, they exchanged info, and they hung up the phone.

In his post-draft season, after a defenceman on Djurgardens IK was sidelined for four months with an injury in training camp, Staffan was given an audition in the Swedish Elite League, the country's top flight, and played well enough in their preseason tournament to stick with the team. That year, on a team where Niklas had already established himself, Staffan played with his older brother for their lone season of hockey together before Niklas left for the NHL. But when the season was over, even after he was nominated for the Swedish Elite League's rookie of the year award, Staffan's perception of himself—and nonexistent NHL expectations—still hadn't shifted. He didn't really hear from the Leafs that season and recognized that he was still a long way away from entering their plans given where he was selected.

A few months later, though, in September 2003, the Leafs participated in the NHL Challenge, a weeklong training camp in Stockholm and Helsinki that included three preseason games, including one against Staffan's—and then Leafs captain Mats Sundin's—hometown club in Djurgarden. The camp, which Staffan knew he wouldn't have been invited to had it been hosted as usual back in Toronto, gave Staffan his first opportunity to showcase himself for the Leafs brass in two of the three games. Though Staffan knew he stood no chance of making the stacked Leafs team, which was about to start its sixth consecutive season as a contender, he came away from the camp pleased with how he played and hopeful for the first time, a week after his 21st birthday, that he might someday be able to give the NHL a go.

"I always felt that I wasn't going to make that phone call and say, 'Hey, [Leafs general manager] John Ferguson, I'm ready to come and give it a chance,'" Staffan said. "I wanted them to show that they thought I was ready. I was lucky enough when they had training camp here because that gave me a very good chance to show who I was."

After returning to Djurgardens for a second season in 2003–04 after the Leafs cut him and a third season in 2004–05 during the NHL's season-long lockout, the Leafs signed Staffan and countryman Alex Steen, whom they picked in the first round of Staffan's draft class in 2002, on August 9, 2005, inviting Staffan to Toronto for the first time.

Though he knew that he wasn't going to make the Leafs out of camp and would have to start with the AHL's Marlies, Staffan lucked out once more when his arrival in the fall of 2005 coincided with the Leafs' AHL affiliate's relocation from St. John's, Newfoundland, to Toronto's Ricoh Coliseum. After playing his first seven professional games in North America under Marlies coach Paul Maurice, Staffan was recalled by Pat

Quinn's Leafs on October 29, 2005, making his NHL debut later that night against the Senators.

"I came over very prepared. I didn't expect to make the NHL at all, but I was coming with the sense that I wanted to learn. I really wanted to develop. I thought it was scary. It was new. There was some big names on that team," Staffan said. "I thought if I someday make the Leafs that will become a dream come true basically, but I saw it as more of an opportunity to become a better hockey player."

Staffan spent most of the season playing on the Leafs' third pairing, bouncing once to the AHL in December before returning and playing with the team through February. Between his debut at the end of October and a final demotion to the Marlies, where he finished the season and played into the AHL playoffs, Staffan got into 34 NHL games.

The following season, though, in the second and last year of his entry-level contract, he spent the full season with the Marlies, winning the team's top defenceman award to earn a two-year contract extension.

Staffan bounced between the AHL and the NHL again in 2007–08, playing a 10-game stint with the Leafs in November and December and an eight-game run in March and April.

After failing to make the Leafs full-time once more in his fourth year with the team in 2008–09, Staffan played the first half of the season with the Marlies before he was claimed off re-entry waivers in February by the Capitals. In Washington, he played three more NHL games before finishing the season with their AHL affiliate, the Hershey Bears, leading the Bears to a Calder Cup title with 12 points in 21 playoff games to lead the AHL's playoffs in scoring by a defenceman.

That off-season, though, the Capitals didn't re-sign him and Staffan signed his third—and eventually final—NHL contract with the Flames, bouncing once more between the NHL and the AHL in 2009–10 and scoring his first and only NHL goal in an October 6 game between the Flames and the Canadiens.

After growing tired of the constant uncertainty and life as an injury-laden NHL defenceman, Kronwall decided to return home in 2010, ending his NHL career at 66 games played across three teams and five seasons. He signed the following year with Djurgardens and played a leading role, logging a team-high 22:50 per game and earning his first invite to Sweden's senior men's national team for the 2011 IIHF World Championship, where he won a silver medal.

He then signed in the KHL, moving to Russia to join Severstal Cherepovets. Early on in that first season in Russia, the hockey world was struck by a catastrophe when a charter flight carrying the Lokomotiv Yaroslavl team to its season opener in Minsk crashed shortly after takeoff on September 7, 2011, killing 44 of the 45 people on board, including all the players on the team's roster, four players from its junior level MHL team, and all three of the team's coaches.

Just a few days before the crash, Staffan's Severstal team had played its final preseason game in Yaroslavl against Lokomotiv. On the other side of the ice was Karlis Skrastins, who he'd played against twice in the NHL; Pavol Demitra, who he'd played against in his debut with the Flames; several others who he'd crossed paths with at various points in his career; and Swedish goaltender Stefan Liv, who he knew personally through years playing against him in the Swedish Elite

League and Swedish junior ranks and with him in various capacities with the national team. (Liv was also quite close with Niklas because the two were both born in 1980, both drafted by the Red Wings in 2000, and Liv played the 2006–07 season in Detroit and Grand Rapids while Niklas was there.)

A few days after the crash, Cherepovets were among the several KHL teams to travel to Arena 2000, Yaroslavl's home rink, for a mass memorial service local authorities said welcomed 100,000 people.

The scene at the arena stuck with Staffan, shaking him. He watched as the family members of those lost crowded around the coffins of their loved ones, their photos placed on top of their caskets laid out in rows, screaming and crying in the silence.

"It was…it was difficult," he said, choking up between words more than a decade later. "It was a tough start to my life in the KHL. Seeing all of their families around the coffins in basically full panic mode, it hits you in a very real way. It's so hard to put words into it actually because it was so surreal. They were hugging the coffins. It's something I'll never forget. Hockey is a small community and I played against a bunch of them. You've shaken their hands at several times. It still hits you even though the only guy I knew personally was Stefan Liv. I was in shock when it happened."

Though the KHL resumed in the days after the crash with minute-long moments of silence before each game and Staffan finished the season with Severstal, playing in his second World Championship for Sweden that spring, he told himself throughout that year that if Lokomotiv were to eventually return to the KHL that he wanted to be a part of it.

When the KHL fulfilled its memorial service promise to bring pro hockey back to the city by relaunching the program in time for the 2012–13 season, Staffan followed through with his own promise to himself and was among the very first players to sign with the team.

"I felt like it was a calling to me, like this was something I needed to do," he said.

In their first season back, he was named one of Yaroslavl's assistant captains and later a KHL All-Star for the first of two times, helping Lokomotiv finish fourth in the KHL's Western Conference with 22 points in 50 games, good for fourth on the team in scoring.

That May, in his third consecutive appearance for Sweden at the world championship, which was held jointly in Stockholm and Helsinki, Staffan was then named captain of the 2013 roster, leading them to a 3–2 upset win over a Canadian team that featured stars like Steven Stamkos and Claude Giroux, and eventually to the gold medal on home soil.

The win was, to that point, the highlight of his career.

"I felt like I won triple gold with that win because it was in my hometown, in my home arena, and I was captain for the team," Staffan said. "It was a moment you'll never forget when we were beating Canada with a superstar team in the quarters and winning that game. We felt like after that there was no way anyone was stopping us."

In the years that followed, though, as Staffan continued to play prominent roles for Sweden internationally on teams filled with NHLers, the real joy of his career became his role with Lokomotiv. Yaroslavl became a second home of sorts, and he a staple of its team.

In 2015–16, his fourth season with the team, he was named Lokomotiv's captain, a rare honour for a non-Russian player—one he says means more to him than twice captaining Sweden's national team.

"This was a good Russian team that has a history of being a top team in the league and to have an import captain is something that's never been heard of in one of those teams before. To be asked that by Russian coach [Alexei Kudashov] as well is something," Staffan said. "I remember I told the coach, 'Good luck with that because the president will never allow it.' I had Tom Rowe, he was the first coach of the team, and he told me he wanted me as captain but the president would say there was no chance of that happening. And I was fine with that. I would act the same with a 'C,' or an 'A,' or nothing. But it wasn't just coming from an import coach who liked an import player, it was coming from a Russian coach who had won in Russia. I was very proud to be asked that."

Staffan went on to captain the team for five seasons. He retired in 2020 at the age of 37, after eight years with Lokomotiv and more than 900 pro games, when his body began to break down.

Lokomotiv quickly brought him on as a development coach, recruiter, and advisor to the head coach and president for the 2020–21 KHL season and beyond. Staff within the Lokomotiv organization talk about Staffan as a huge figure in their community and the history of their franchise.

At 9 PM local time on Valentine's Day 2021, he is back home in the suburbs of Stockholm a day after making a late-night flight back from Lokomotiv, having just tucked his two sons, Maximillian, age seven, and Alexander, age four, into bed. When Lokomotiv asked him to stay on, he made sure that his arrangement with the team allowed him to live at home because it was important to him that his oldest son, who was starting his first year of school, be educated in Sweden. Though he never made it as a full-time NHL player, he has fond memories of his three seasons in Toronto. He credits Sundin for his mentorship of the team's Swedes and considers Steen a good friend to this day. He knew then that the odds weren't in his favour, so he doesn't hold any resentment, and insists Maurice, Quinn, and Ferguson all treated him well.

"[Steen] came the same year and he was a big prospect, the first-rounder, and I was, you know, I was picked in the very last round. So we were at a different spot. He knew he was going to get his chance and I knew that I was going to have to really prove myself because everyone knows it's a lot of politics in the game of hockey, especially over there. So I knew I had an uphill climb," Staffan said. "It's funny how you kind of take different paths. I was extremely happy to do the things I did in North America, but I felt like whenever I was close I got a big injury that sent me back and I got tired of that up and down. I felt I needed a change and when I went back to Europe, I felt I took another step."

He's thankful that when he made the jump it was to Toronto and not St. John's. He remembers fondly his apartment at 10 Queens Quay, just across from the Westin Harbour Castle Hotel on Lake Ontario, and less fondly the criticism he received from Leafs fans during a tumultuous time in the organization's history on his 500-metre walks to the Air Canada Centre.

"To be in the AHL and the NHL in the same city in Toronto, which is one of the best, coolest cities in the world, I was really fortunate to have that opportunity and it made it not a difficult decision to come. But we had a bad stretch and people were saying how bad we were when I walked to the rink, so I started driving," Staffan said, laughing. "I felt I didn't need all that mouth rolling. It was such a great experience because of how everyone is involved in the team and what's going on, but I was the sixth defenceman when I was up, I didn't play any big minutes or special teams, I was basically filling in when someone was injured, yet people recognized someone from the Leafs and they weren't happy with the team's results."

The best years of his career were in Yaroslavl, though. In the prime of his career with Lokomotiv, he was offered several one-way contracts to return to the NHL.

He turned them each down.

"I felt like I wasn't ready," he said of the timing of each of those offers. "I was considered a big player in the KHL at the time, and I wasn't ready to come back and be on a one-way contract, which meant at that time that there were several one-way contracts in the minors. I wasn't ready to go there to play 8 to 10 minutes as a No. 6–7 defenceman or sit and eat popcorn in the stands. I really wanted to contribute, and I felt I did that in the KHL."

Though his career never looked like his big brother's, he's proud of the one he made for himself.

"I think Nik was a very intelligent hockey player. He was known for his big hits, but he was a heck of a player. You don't play a decade and a half in the NHL as a top-four defenceman unless you're a good player. But I believe we played different. He was throwing bigger hits and he was a good skater. I played I think when I moved to the KHL more of a skilled hockey than he was. I was pointing the power play and I didn't have a big shot, but I knew how to play to set up my teammates," Staffan said proudly.

On top of his role with Lokomotiv, he's also now a TV analyst on Saturdays for the league he used to play in, now called the Swedish Hockey League. In both jobs, he has begun to look at the game—and the late-round NHL prospects who are now trying to carve out a career path of their own—through a different lens.

"I see a lot of players coming up that are very much alike. They're all steeped in the same form so to speak," Staffan said. "I feel like I've always analyzed the game and I think in Sweden there's a lot of small details that they still haven't caught up with. It's 'this stick is pointed the wrong way, he needs to take this angle.' Small details make a huge difference in the game of hockey these days because it's so fast."

And even as the talent of the players he works with in Russia and dissects in Sweden rises, Staffan wants to impart lessons learned from his career, and that flooded soccer field with Nik, on a future generation of draft hopefuls.

"The one thing in Sweden that I think lacks is actually the game of hockey. I feel like the hockey sense has almost become lower. Every kid has a shooting ramp, a skating coach, and a skills coach. They can do all of these cool tricks. But when I was growing up and when I was a kid, all I wanted to do was play. I never had a shooting ramp. I was playing one-on-one against my brothers, and we were always fighting and I was always bigger and stronger than Nik but he was better than me," Staffan said. "You learn a lot from that. You learn how to protect the puck, the balance, where to place the puck so that he can't reach it, and so on. I don't see that nowadays from kids. I see a lot of individual skill. I hope to help fill in the gaps. I hope to be a part of what comes next."

11

THE JOHN FERGUSON JR. ERA

JOHN FERGUSON JR. is sitting at his son's lacrosse practice inside a quiet Boston arena. His phone is to his ear as he tells stories of his life in hockey, and of the people and moments that shaped it. When he arrives at his four-and-a-half seasons as general manager of the Leafs, he can't help but lament.

"We should have rebuilt," he says. "And ultimately it became self-evident that that's what had to happen. It just took longer to get there."

Though he doesn't say as much, it's clear that the way he is perceived in Toronto still wears on him more than 13 years after his dismissal. But when the conversation pivots to the four Leafs drafts he oversaw, his tone shifts. In place of attempts to set the record straight, and stories about the politics of the gig or missed opportunities, he speaks of discoveries, of philosophy, and of success stories.

"Future NHL games are being won and lost on today's scouting battlefields," he says, reciting a mantra he admits all his colleagues have heard over the years. "For me, scouting xenophobes make desirable opponents because they leave gaps in their coverage, if not consciously then subconsciously. Those who keep a broader perspective can make hay."

The draft and everything that comes with it—its process, its research, its recruiting, its theory, its analytics, its player evaluation, and ultimately its study—is where Ferguson Jr.'s roots are. The most pivotal moments of Ferguson Jr.'s career have happened on draft weekend. Job interviews. A hotel elevator conversation. The selections and trades that he made himself or had a hand in for six different NHL clubs. Though his time in Toronto took on a life and reputation of its own, his track record leading the Leafs through the 2004–07 drafts stands the test of time.

FERGUSON JR. WAS born on July 7, 1967, in Montreal, the summer before his father, John Ferguson Sr., began his pursuit of his third of five Stanley Cups with the Canadiens. Though Ferguson Sr. was a two-time All-Star and runner-up for the Calder Trophy, he was known more as superstar Jean Beliveau's protector and racked up more than 100 penalty minutes in each of his eight seasons in the NHL, all in Montreal.

After retiring from his playing career in 1971, Ferguson Sr. served as an assistant coach with Team Canada for its 1972 Summit Series victory over the Soviet Union. In the four decades that followed, he was a head coach and general manager of the Rangers and Jets (a team he oversaw in the WHA through its merger into the NHL), director of player personnel for the Senators, and scout and special assistant to the general manager with the Sharks, a role he filled while battling prostate cancer until his passing in 2007.

So Ferguson Jr. grew up in the sport, bouncing from city to city with his dad; mom, Joan; and three siblings, Chris, Catherine, and Joanne, before settling in Winnipeg for his junior high and high school years.

As Ferguson Jr. tried to carve out his own path as a hockey player, he fielded the same question over and over.

"What's it like having a father who played and then later on became a manager?"

His answer was always the same.

"To be honest, I've never had any other father so I'm not sure what the differences are."

For a long time, Ferguson Jr. struggled to find an identity that wasn't tied to his dad's. They shared everything. A love for hockey. A love for horse racing. A love for lacrosse. It wasn't lost on him, either, how lucky he was to grow up around some of the best hockey players of the 1970s and 1980s. In Winnipeg, he developed his father's passion for player evaluation on frequent trips south to watch the University of North Dakota. He sat and listened as his dad made some of the WHA's and NHL's first inroads into Europe, recruiting players like Anders Hedberg, Ulf Nilsson, and Thomas Steen to North America. That upbringing shaped the way he eventually approached his jobs in hockey. When his dad gave him life lessons, he listened, admiring him for his work ethic and attention to detail.

For a long time, though, Ferguson Sr. cast a long shadow. The name "John Ferguson Jr." came with immediate recognition. To one person, he was the son of one of the toughest players to ever play. To the next, he was the son of the boss of the Jets. And for all that his dad gave him, those comparisons also made him squeamish.

"I tried to make my hockey résumé unassailable from those who might criticize for nepotism. I tried to make my path bulletproof," Ferguson said. "I tried to look out for myself, to clean up my own messes, and that lesson of establishing your own independence was instilled in me as much by my mother as my father."

Even when the time came for his own draft day in June 1985, shortly after he'd finished his tier-two junior career and shortly before he was set to arrive at Providence College for his freshman year, the father-son ties tightened when the Canadiens used their final pick of the 1985 draft to select Ferguson Jr. 247th overall.

At Providence, Ferguson Jr. struggled on the ice, turning his focus off it into a pursuit of a degree in business administration. As a freshman and sophomore, he wasn't a regular in the Friars lineup. But he excelled in the classroom, becoming an Academic All-American and later graduating magna cum laude. Coincidentally, his time in the Schneider Arena press box as a healthy scratch early on also helped him forge relationships with the people who'd become two of his biggest mentors in the sport—Brian Burke and Lou Lamoriello. Burke, a Providence grad himself, took his first job in the

NHL as director of hockey operations for the Vancouver Canucks in the 1987–88 season, when Ferguson Jr. was a junior with the Friars. But before that, Burke worked at a law firm in Boston and as an agent, did some NCAA recruiting, and provided colour analysis for Providence College's broadcasts. While at Providence, Ferguson Jr. also ran into Burke at Boston's Logan International Airport one Christmas while they both waited for a flight to Minneapolis, where Ferguson Jr. had to catch a connecting flight to Winnipeg. Ferguson Jr. developed a relationship with Lamoriello because he was Providence College's director of player personnel for his first two years at the program (after more than a decade as the Friars' head coach before Ferguson Jr.'s arrival). Lamoriello took his first NHL gig during Ferguson Jr.'s sophomore season at Providence when the New Jersey Devils hired him as team president.

Though Ferguson Jr. debated following in Burke's and Lamoriello's footsteps by pursuing law school when he graduated (the latter actually advised him to do just that instead of pursuing a playing career), even taking the LSAT, a strong senior year with the Friars was enough for him to pursue pro hockey and earn a contract with the Canadiens' farm team.

At the end of Ferguson Jr.'s second of four seasons in the AHL (three with the Canadiens organization and one with the Senators' affiliate in New Haven), Burke was in Vancouver and reached out when he was looking to hire an intern for the Canucks' office.

"I said, 'Well, I'm still trying to be a player,'" Ferguson Jr. remembered, chuckling to himself about the interaction. "So that was an indication of his assessment of where he thought I might be going or not going as a pro."

In his final year of pro hockey in New Haven, Ferguson Jr. eventually sat down with Don MacAdam, the team's head coach, for a frank discussion about whether he should pursue law school or another contract.

"If you stop playing now, you'll be done for a long time," MacAdam told him.

Ferguson Jr., recognizing the reality of that, tried to keep his options open, applying for law schools throughout the rest of the season before spending the summer training in Amherstburg, Ontario, with fellow journeyman Warren Rychel in case he got another contract.

When the right one never came, Ferguson Jr. moved back to Boston to attend Suffolk University Law School, immersing himself so much in his education that he didn't have time to regret leaving his playing career behind.

While in law school for three years, Ferguson Jr. then got his first opportunities on the other side of the sport, working part-time as a scout for the Senators, where Ferguson Sr. was the team's director of player personnel, and interning at the NHL's offices.

He also reached out to several teams about managerial roles, but there were no fits. After passing the bar exam in Massachusetts and graduating from law school, he then interviewed with several agencies, including hockey giant Newport, which had represented him during his playing career. He chose Lawton Sport and Financial, run by former first overall NHL draft pick Brian Lawton out of Minneapolis, because it was a boutique agency that didn't have anyone on the East Coast and he wanted to negotiate contracts immediately (instead of recruiting Midget-aged players in the role that was offered to him with Newport). Under Lawton, Ferguson Jr. sat in living rooms with top prospects like Hal Gill.

"It gave me perspective of the players, and the clients, and their parents. It pushed me into areas that I was not altogether that comfortable with. It's sink or swim. You've got to get out there and live up to the sales job," Ferguson Jr. said.

After a year as an agent, some of those people he'd reached out to after he graduated began to circle back. Ferguson Jr., knowing that if he stayed as an agent for much longer that it might be a decade before he got out of that world if his client base grew, took the interviews. Those opportunities really began to come to a head at the 1997 NHL draft, which was held on June 21 of that year in Pittsburgh. Two weeks before the draft, the St. Louis Blues had hired Larry Pleau as their new general manager and Pleau reached out to Ferguson Jr. because he already had his résumé. Dave Taylor, who'd taken over as Kings general manager that April, reached out for the same reasons. A couple of weeks after the draft, Ken Holland, who'd just been named general manager of the Red Wings, also called him about an opportunity after spending a day discussing the team's future with Scotty Bowman. But it was Ferguson Jr.'s 7 AM meeting on the Sunday after the draft with Pleau that stuck with him. Later that day, when he ran into Lamoriello in the hotel elevator, he asked his mentor's advice.

"'Lou, I've got an opportunity on the management side and I've met with two teams. What do you think?" Ferguson Jr. said.

Lamoriello deadpanned him.

"Get out of that ass-kissing business as soon as you can," he answered with his typical succinctness as he stepped out of the elevator without looking back.

Ferguson Jr. took his advice and agreed to take the Blues job a few days after the draft. When Holland called him about the Red Wings gig, he had to decline.

Ferguson Jr., then 30, joined the Blues as assistant general manager. Pleau became an even bigger mentor than Lamoriello and Burke had, second only to his dad, placing a lot on his plate (including director of hockey operations for the Blues and president and general manager of the Worcester IceCats, their AHL franchise).

After six seasons with the Blues, that opportunity turned into another at another draft, this time in 2003 in Nashville.

Leading into the weekend, Pat Quinn, who then held both the Leafs' general manager and head coach roles, reached out to Pleau to see if he could interview Ferguson Jr. in his search for his own replacement as general manager. Ferguson Jr., who'd already had one interview for a general manager opportunity with the Sharks, interviewed with the Leafs across several stages, first over the phone and then twice in Toronto with Maple Leafs Sports and Entertainment president and CEO Richard Peddie.

After sorting out the paperwork and delaying the announcement due to scheduling conflicts with Peddie, Quinn, and the Raptors, Ferguson Jr. was officially introduced as the Leafs' 12th general manager on August 29, 2003, at the age of 36, just a week before the team flew to Sweden for their training camp.

He took over an aging Leafs team that featured stars like Mats Sundin, Joe Nieuwendyk, Gary Roberts, Owen Nolan, Alexander Mogilny, and Ed Belfour, with a payroll of more than $62 million (sixth highest in the league at the time) and high expectations.

"It was an exciting period of time and without question I felt ready to do what needed to be done," Ferguson Jr. said.

With the NHL and NHLPA's collective bargaining agreement set to expire, he approached that first season intent on contending. Though nobody on the team or league side expected there to be a full-season work stoppage the following year, or the institution of a hard salary cap, the Leafs allocated a percentage of their earnings to his budget, which was indicative of their willingness to contend and in line with the cut of revenue the league's other best teams were likely to spend—or at least not all that far behind the Red Wings and the Rangers, who were spending closer to $80 million on their payrolls.

Ferguson Jr. felt that his budget and his directive were reasonable and sensible, given that the Leafs were at the tail end of a contending window.

"We had a pretty good sense of what our club was made of. I did feel that there should be a couple of years to push it and get it done before the aging process was going to take over. And frankly, thereafter I had hoped and planned to enter more of a rebuild," Ferguson Jr. said.

In advance of the 2004 trade deadline, the Leafs were neck-and-neck in a race for the top of the Eastern Conference standings, and Ferguson committed to upgrading the roster.

In late February, he began an aggressive pursuit of a top defenceman, engaging in frequent discussions with Rangers general manager Glen Sather, who was selling future Hall of Famer Brian Leetch, and Capitals general manager George McPhee, who was shopping All-Star Sergei Gonchar, the league's highest-scoring defenceman that season.

"George was literally going day-to-day saying, 'I'm going to trade that guy tomorrow, how about this guy?' And he had them all lined up. And I was in on Gonchar extensively," Ferguson Jr. said.

Because Leetch had a year remaining on his contract and Gonchar was a pending free agent, Ferguson Jr. made the deal with Sather, trading a 2004 first-round pick (which became Kris Chucko, who played just two NHL games), a 2005 second-round pick (which became Michael Sauer, who played 98 games across parts of three NHL seasons), and prospects Maxim Kondratiev and Jarkko Immonen to the Rangers for Leetch. That same day, March 3, Gonchar was dealt to the Bruins for a first and a second and Shaone Morrisonn. (Gonchar later signed with the Penguins as a free agent.) A week later, on deadline day, Ferguson Jr. then dealt a fourth-round pick in the 2005 draft to the Carolina Hurricanes for their longtime captain and one of the league's all-time leading scorers, 40-year-old Ron Francis, who registered 10 points in 12 games for the Leafs down the stretch before retiring after their playoff run.

The Leafs finished that season with a then franchise record 45 wins and 103 points, three points back of the Lightning (who went on to win the Stanley Cup) for first in the East. They defeated the Senators in seven games in the conference quarterfinals before falling to the Flyers in six games in the conference semifinals.

When the 2004 draft, held in Raleigh, North Carolina, arrived, Ferguson Jr. was without his first- and second rounders (the first was his own doing, the second was dealt for defenceman Glen Wesley the season before he was hired). Still, through his experience scouting for the Senators for three years and helping to run the Blues' draft board for six more, Ferguson Jr.'s first draft with the Leafs was really his 10th. The Leafs didn't make their first selection, Justin Pogge, until 90th overall. The result was Ferguson Jr.'s worst draft as Leafs general manager, with only Pogge and 187th overall pick Robbie Earl emerging to play NHL games among the Leafs' seven picks in Rounds 3–9.

He never got the second year out of Leetch that he'd spent his 2004 and 2005 draft capital to acquire, either, because the final year of Leetch's contract was lost by the looming 2004–05 lockout.

Though the lockout dramatically changed the Leafs' trajectory, nudging them into a decade-long struggle, it also gave Ferguson Jr. a full year to focus on one thing: the NHL draft. The Leafs launched into an "extensive" amateur scouting process. After a full year of travelling the hockey world to scout the 2005 draft, the draft was then pushed back from its planned June 25 date to July 30, and moved from the Senators' arena, the Corel Centre, to Ottawa's Westin Hotel. The draft itself underwent a format overhaul, too. Its length was reduced from nine rounds to seven rounds, and it was closed to the public for the first time since 1980, with only NHL Central Scouting's 20 highest-ranked prospects attending in person.

Because no season was played, the draft lottery was also revamped and turned into a spectacle that became known as the Crosby sweepstakes. Under the new collective bargaining agreement, each of the league's 30 teams were given weighted lottery odds according to a combination of their playoff performances and their first overall picks from the previous three seasons. Three lottery balls were awarded to teams with no playoff appearances and no first overall picks from 2002 to '04. Two lottery balls were assigned to teams with one playoff appearance or one first overall pick in that timespan. All other teams received one lottery ball. After each team was drawn and the first-round order was complete, a snake draft was established so that the team that picked first in the first round picked last in the second round—and so on. The Leafs received one of the 48 total balls assigned, giving them a 2.1 percent chance at first overall. They landed the 21st overall selection.

Though Ferguson was still without his second- and fourth-round picks, the Leafs' 2005 class was a success, producing four NHL players—including two of the draft's home runs—with their six selections.

They picked their first of those home runs in the first round, selecting goaltender Tuukka Rask.

"Tuukka was a starter as an underage with Ilves' under-18 team and had a real big year that year, but his actual draft year, if you went solely by it, some teams wouldn't have taken him in the first round, for whatever reason," Ferguson Jr. said. "I still believe there is a sentiment to this day that says, 'Is that a solid use of a first-round pick? Are you going to realize the benefits of it?' I don't subscribe to that theory.

There's no question that if you can identify that player, acquire the player with a first-round pick, and then be committed to developing that player, you can realize some real big returns. Carey Price. Roberto Luongo. If you really look at the number of first-round starters, it's probably more than people would think anecdotally. And Tuukka we were very aware of. We saw the talent level and felt without question that he was the pick at 21."

The Leafs' second home run came much later, when they selected defenceman Anton Stralman (who went on to become one of the draft's best defencemen) in the seventh round.

"You cannot maximize the entire value of your draft if you take players earlier than they need to be taken. That does inherently mean you're going to assume some level of risk that that player that you want may not be available when you think he needs to be taken. But if you continue to take players quote-unquote earlier than they would otherwise need to be chosen, you're minimizing the ceiling of your entire draft," Ferguson explained of his approach to late-round choices. "Stralman's a prime example of attempting to extract value deep in the draft."

Into August, though, as the Leafs prepared to exit the lockout for the 2005–06 season, their roster wasn't anything like the one that pursued a Stanley Cup before the stoppage. Belfour was 40 and all of Nieuwendyk, Roberts, Mogilny, and Nolan were gone—but their expectations didn't adjust accordingly.

"The word *rebuild* was non-grata. It wasn't going to be used internally or externally. I think that that was a mistake," Ferguson Jr. said. "And I remember George McPhee saying about the challenges and unknown of entering a rebuild, 'The problem is when you start going south in the standings, you don't know where the bottom is, and that's very challenging.' So I don't say it without appreciating the risks and the realities at some attempts at a rebuild on the fly."

After sputtering to a slow start, the Leafs got hot late in the season, finishing 9–1–2 in their final 12 games to finish two points shy of the playoffs, missing the postseason for the first time since 1998. A week later, Quinn and assistant coach Rick Ley were relieved of their duties. A couple of weeks after that, Marlies head coach Paul Maurice was named as Quinn's replacement. And a month later the 2006 NHL draft was held on June 24 in Vancovuer.

On Day 1 of the draft, Ferguson Jr. traded Rask, who'd just won the 2006 World Juniors' top goaltender award leading Finland to a bronze medal, to the Boston Bruins for Andrew Raycroft, who, before the lockout, won the Calder Trophy when he posted a .926 save percentage across 57 games, and four years before that had won the CHL's goaltender of the year award. The trade went on to overshadow the draft, living in infamy as Raycroft bounced from team to team in the years that followed before departing for Europe in 2012 at the age of 32, while Rask became a perennial Vezina Trophy contender as one of the league's best goalies.

"We'd have been far better off not making the trade for Raycroft. And Raycroft was a good goaltender. But without question the returns on that trade were shorter term. And credit to Tuukka and the team that acquired him, that committed to developing him the right way behind Tim Thomas," Ferguson Jr. said. "Would he have pushed through no matter where he was? I think he would have. But I don't think anybody can argue with the development of Tuukka Rask with Boston."

Out of the shadow of the Rask–Raycroft trade, the 2006 draft became one of the Leafs' best ever, producing six NHL players and more than 2,600 NHL games played with just seven picks (the most games played by a Leafs draft class since 1987, when they hit on six of 12 picks).

Maybe their least successful pick of the 2006 class—at least relative to the slot—was their first, Jiri Tlusty, at 13th overall, and even then, though future star Claude Giroux was taken nine picks later, five of the players picked between Tlusty and Giroux never became full-time NHL players while Tlusty played 450 games for four teams.

In the second round, the Leafs picked Nikolay Kulemin, who went on to have a 30-goal season for the team. After trading their third-round pick (which became forward Tony Lagerstrom, who never played in the NHL) to the Blackhawks for two fourth-round picks, the Leafs used those two picks to draft goaltender James Reimer and defenceman Korbinian Holzer.

Reimer, who was a backup in the WHL with the Red Deer Rebels in his draft year, proved to be a find—and someone Ferguson Jr. credits Leafs goalie scout Mike Palmaeteer for identifying.

"Reimer projected to be a starter the very next year, which he became and which we factored into what we considered to be another good bet on an upside goaltender who possessed what I like to call prototypical No. 1 starting goaltender size. And if he's not a slam-dunk No. 1 to this day, he has certainly been as good as any tandem goaltender to this day, and that represents value in the draft," Ferguson Jr. said.

Two rounds later, after moving two seventh-round picks (both of which also never played NHL games) to the Coyotes to move up into the sixth round, the Leafs selected forward Viktor Stalberg, who later played one season in Toronto before he was dealt to Chicago to acquire forward Kris Versteeg.

Later in the sixth round, with their final pick of the draft, the Leafs also selected Leo Komarov, who, after years spent in Finland and Russia, played five seasons for the Leafs, including three as an assistant captain.

"We did know when we drafted Komarov that what we were projecting to get was going to be a hard-nosed, two-way bottom-six forward with the ability to agitate and make plays offensively. He was not a prototypical size, strength, upside draft pick. But when you consider that he was a sixth rounder, we felt very comfortable with that risk-reward assessment at that selection," Ferguson Jr. said. "Without question, his additional time in Europe allowed him to grow, he became a captain, and he matured physically and mentally as a person and a professional before he came over."

The following season, though, played out much like the previous one had. The Leafs, intent on clawing their way to a playoff spot, came up just short, famously missing the playoffs by one point on the last game of the season when the Islanders defeated the Devils in a shootout to secure the final spot.

Ferguson Jr. then made another significant move on the opening day of the draft, this time in Columbus in 2007, trading the team's 2007 first-rounder (the 13th overall pick, which became NHLer Lars Eller), 2007 second-rounder (which became journeyman Aaron Palushaj), and 2009 fourth-rounder (which became NHLer Craig Smith) to the Sharks in exchange for goaltender Vesa Toskala and winger Mark Bell. Without his first- and second-rounders for the second time as general manager, Ferguson Jr. did well with what he'd left himself, selecting three NHL players in Rounds 3–7 and finding another late-round gem in seventh-round pick Carl Gunnarsson.

"I remember having conversations with our guys from Europe and guys that cross over to Europe, whether it's Thommie Bergman or Dave Morrison, and in that instance with Gunnarsson, that was the same draft as [Frazer] McLaren, the big kid from Winnipeg that San Jose took in the seventh round, and we liked him and I probably should have taken one of them a round earlier because I wanted both but we thought that McLaren might get through and we were going to invite him to camp, so we took Gunnarsson. But we were certainly not complaining about who we took," Ferguson Jr. said.

Again, though, the picks didn't become the story when Ferguson Jr.'s big draft trade didn't work out. In August of that off-season, Bell pleaded no contest to drunk driving causing injury and hit and run, two charges which stemmed from an accident he caused when he rear-ended a pick-up truck at a stop sign while going an estimated 100 kilometres an hour on Labor Day weekend 2006. The league also suspended him for the first 15 games of the following season with the Leafs and he was placed on waivers by the team a year later. When Toskala struggled in his first season as a starter, the Leafs finally cratered out, going from fringe playoff team to the bottom of the standings.

And by Christmas, Ferguson Jr. began to see the writing on the wall and wonder if changes were imminent. He was fired on January 22, with the Leafs sitting 19–22–8 and 14th in the Eastern Conference, and replaced by former Leafs general manager Cliff Fletcher.

His time with the Leafs remains the one period of his career filled with the most regrets.

"In training camp that year, there was a media availability with Paul Maurice and myself, and Paul felt and expressed that it should be a playoff team or there should be changes. And I think that was an honest expression of the perception, which became reality. I'm not sure it needed to be expressed publicly prior to the season but I do think it's probably what he'd heard from the board, and he was merely stating what he felt was our reality as a club. We were all connected in that respect. Whether or not that was a fair assessment by those above us really doesn't matter because that's what it was," Ferguson Jr. said.

In the years that followed Ferguson Jr.'s dismissal, he took upper management positions with the Sharks, Bruins, and Coyotes. He helped successfully retool on the fly and extend contending windows with each of the first two and hopes to help the third through a complete rebuild.

He wishes he'd been able—and allowed—to do in Toronto what he's now trying to do in Arizona: start over. But he wasn't, and the Leafs continued to trade picks and young assets to push for the playoffs in the years that followed his termination under his successors, including his old mentor Burke and another of Burke's mentees, Dave Nonis.

"Without question, there was more in place than many let on at the time, but that does require time and sometimes you've got to be able to keep your job to see things through. In that instance, I was not able to do that. It was a challenging time handling the different agendas, pressures, and expectations," Ferguson Jr said. "We as an organization missed an opportunity to proactively embrace a true reset, if not a rebuild, that ultimately became unavoidable."

To this day, though Ferguson Jr. has many regrets, he's proud of what he was able to accomplish in Toronto, winning the team's last playoff series for more than a decade and guiding the franchise through an unprecedented lockout and into the salary cap era.

He's most proud of his record at the draft, though.

While the Leafs made just three of their eight picks in the first two rounds of the four drafts he oversaw, some of which was his own doing and some of which wasn't, 15 of the 26 picks Ferguson Jr. did make—an impressive 58 percent—played in NHL games.

12

THE LUKE
SCHENN PICK

"SO, UH, THE Leafs haven't won the Cup since 1967;
what are you going to do to change that?"

Not even two or three minutes after pulling his new
blue-and-white jersey over his head for the very first time,
that's the first thing Luke Schenn remembers being asked.
He remembers it, and not the rest, because it snapped him
out of his haze.

Holy man, this is crazy, he thought to himself.

Thirteen years later, on an off day between two April
games with the Tampa Bay Lightning, his seventh NHL club,
Schenn is able to laugh about that moment. It was, he admits,
his first eye-opener to everything that would follow and the
pressures that came with being the 18-year-old face of a fragile
franchise.

Schenn's place in Leafs history was determined more by others than by him. That moment set the table.

THE LEAFS ARRIVED at the 2008 NHL draft in Ottawa (which would be re-awarded its position as host after having lost the 2005 draft to the lockout) with the seventh overall pick, five months after firing general manager John Ferguson Jr. and naming long time executive Cliff Fletcher as general manager for a second time (he'd previously held the Leafs' top job from 1991 to '97), this time on an interim basis.

Schenn arrived in Ottawa for draft day as NHL Central Scouting's fifth-ranked North American prospect. His hockey trajectory to that point had followed the linear path of the typical top prospect. He was born in Saskatoon as the oldest child of Rita and Jeff Schenn's four kids, with younger brother Brayden and younger sisters Madison and Macy to follow. He and Brayden were just 21 months apart and took to hockey immediately, with Luke gravitating toward defence and Brayden to forward. As children, they both became stars for the local Saskatoon Redwings. As teenagers, they became the same for the Bantam AAA Saskatoon Generals and Minor Midget AAA Saskatoon Contacts.

In 2004, Luke was drafted 20th overall in the WHL's Bantam draft by the Kelowna Rockets. After playing his 15-year-old 2004–05 season with the Contacts, he joined the Rockets for the home stretch of their season once his had concluded. Though he didn't get into games for them into the playoffs, the Rockets billeted him with Ingrid and Barry Davidson so that he could be around assistant captain Shea Weber, who

The Luke Schenn who pulled this Leafs jersey over his head for the first time
had no idea what awaited him in his career in Toronto, nor of the glory
he'd find wearing a different blue-and-white jersey long after he'd left.
(AP Photo/The Canadian Press, Fred Chartrand)

was in the midst of his final season in the WHL, had won gold for Canada at the world juniors that year, and was already two years removed from being drafted in the second round by the Nashville Predators. When Weber made the leap to the NHL in 2005–06, Luke took over his bedroom and his role as the backbone of the Rockets blue line, posting 11 points in 60 games as a 16-year-old and serving as an assistant captain for Team Canada West at the under-17 world championships that year. The following year, he added another 29 points and 139 penalty minutes as a 17-year-old and scored three goals in six games with Team Canada at under-18 worlds. In his third full season in the WHL in his NHL draft year, Luke then made Team Canada for a third consecutive year, this time at the under-20 world juniors, where he too won gold as the team's fourth-youngest player.

Those three years in major junior (where most other draft-eligible players only had two) and three appearances in prominent roles for Canada on the international stage thrust Luke into the spotlight.

In the lead-up to the draft, Luke interviewed with the Leafs a couple of times, meeting with Fletcher and head amateur scout Dave Morrison in-season, at the combine, and again once more after it. But the Leafs never showed preferential treatment and he didn't feel like they were any more interested in him than the other teams he met with. And despite his high NHL Central Scouting slotting, there was also a ton of confusion about how the draft would play out at the top. Steven Stamkos, who'd just scored 58 goals in 61 games for the OHL's Sarnia Sting, was expected to go first overall to the Lightning, who'd retained the top pick in the lottery after their league-worst finish. After that, though, Luke was among a handful of defenceman who were expected to be picked in the next few selections.

By the time he'd taken his seat—flanked by Rita, Jeff, Brayden, Madison, Macy, his grandparents, the Davidsons, a couple of aunts and uncles, and his agents, Don Meehan and Craig Oster of Newport Sports Management—Luke felt like he was walking into it blind.

"If you look at the draft, it was crazy," Luke said. "You had [Drew] Doughty, [Alex] Pietrangelo, [Zach] Bogosian, Tyler Myers, so there was a bunch of different guys within the same grouping."

After the Lightning took Stamkos first, Doughty, Bogosian, and Pietrangelo were drafted in quick succession. Then the Islanders were up with the fifth overall pick when everything on the draft floor, and TSN's broadcast of it, paused in anticipation of a trade. Before anything was announced in-house at Scotiabank Place (now the Canadian Tire Centre), TSN's Darren Dreger broke the news on the broadcast while Leafs brass huddled at the Islanders table.

"Alright James [Duthie], I just spoke with Leafs general manager Cliff Fletcher and he confirms that the Toronto Maple Leafs have made a trade with the New York Islanders. He wouldn't get into specifics before pushing me aside, other than to say that they will swap picks five and seven," Dreger said.

Seconds later, as boos rained down, NHL commissioner Gary Bettman stepped to the podium to make it official.

"Bear with me on this one. The New York Islanders trade pick No. 5 in this year's draft to Toronto," Bettman said as the boos ramped up, this time for the rival Leafs. "There's more!" he continued. "For pick No. 7 in this year's draft and, at the New York Islanders' option, either pick No. 60 this year and Toronto's third-round pick next year or pick No. 68 this year and Toronto's second-round pick in 2009."

Back on the broadcast, as Bettman announced the deal, host Gord Miller spoke of the pick as the highest one the Leafs had made since drafting Scott Thornton third in 1989, predicting that they'd take Luke and regaling with stories of Fletcher flying through snowstorms to see him play in Kelowna. His analysts, led by Pierre McGuire and Bob McKenzie, lauded the coming pick.

"Hey, I never cheer for anybody, I don't care who wins or loses, [but] Toronto wins big here!" said McGuire. "This is huge for the Toronto Maple Leafs and their organization going forward. This is the start of their rebuild and you couldn't build it on better shoulders than Luke Schenn's. When you can get a player like Luke Schenn, you just go crazy as a scout. This is a franchise player. Barring injury, what a career he will have for the Maple Leafs!"

Back in the crowd, Meehan gave his client a nudge and a wink as the Leafs made their way to the stage to make it official. Luke adjusted his black and grey tie over his belt and smiled as Leafs director of player personnel Mike Penny stepped to the podium.

"The Toronto Maple Leafs are proud to select with their first pick in this year's draft, from the Kelowna Rockets, Luke Schenn."

As he lifted out of his seat, the haze started immediately.

"To finally hear my name called, it was an incredible experience with a sold-out building," Luke said all these years later. "You go up on the podium and you're not honestly even sure who's hand you're shaking. It's just a whirlwind."

LUKE'S SECOND "WELCOME TO TORONTO" moment came a couple months later. The draft set the stage with all the weight McGuire metaphorically put on his shoulders before his name had even been called, and with that first question that came minutes later. Then came the Leafs rookie tournament in Kitchener against the Penguins, Panthers, and Senators.

"I think my first game I was a little bit too nervous and trying to go out there to do too much and I didn't have a very good showing. I remember going down to the lobby the next day to grab a newspaper and they were roasting me pretty good in the paper and that's when it was like, 'Holy smokes, this is my second taste of the Toronto media,'" Luke said. "So after that I actually never read a paper or listened to the sports radio there."

That pressure never really faded, either. It was sown early, and it was tightened again and again as the weight of the Leafs' fledgling franchise, a franchise that had missed the playoffs in three straight years out of the lockout and into his selection, pushed down on him. In Luke's first training camp, new Leafs head coach Ron Wilson, who was hired 10 days before the team picked at the draft, then told his new rookie—and the press—that the only way he was going to make the team was if he could play in the team's top four.

After starting camp as the 10th defenceman on the depth chart, Luke worked his way onto the opening night roster, ramping up those expectations even further. Nine games later, after playing the third-most minutes on the team (21:34 per game, including more than 25 minutes in the third and fourth games of his career) to start the year—and two weeks before his 19th birthday—Wilson and Fletcher told Luke to start looking for a permanent place to stay.

The first offer came from Leafs assistant general manager Joe Nieuwendyk. But Nieuwendyk lived in Oakville, a suburb west of the city. Luke didn't have a car and there weren't any other players out there who could've helped him make the commute in for skates. Several other players also offered to move him in with their wives and families, including veteran goalie Curtis Joseph, who'd signed a one-year contract to return to the Leafs for a second time for what would be his last season in the NHL. But Joseph had four kids and he too lived in the suburbs.

So an 18-year-old Luke declined each offer and instead found a place on Queen's Quay next to the Westin Harbour Castle Hotel, a few hundred metres south of the then named Air Canada Centre on Lake Ontario.

A couple months later, his whirlwind rookie season got another new face, one who could take a little bit of the attention away from him, when the team's 10-month search for a permanent general manager finished with a late November press conference to introduce Brian Burke as the team's new boss.

But as Luke settled into his new home—and its giant spotlight—he always felt like he was on a bit of an island.

"It was my first time living by myself and I kind of just had to figure it out on the fly. There were like no other young guys on the team at that time too. Now you come into the league and there's a handful of rookies on every team. When I came into the league, there were really no other young guys. Everyone was married. The only other single guy on the team was Jeff Finger and I hung out with him quite a lot, but I was 18 and he was 29," Luke said with a laugh of his rookie season. "It was interesting. We were kind of in a rebuild even though we were an older, veteran team."

That veteran team included a 41-year-old Joseph, 34-year-old Jason Blake, 33-year-old Jamal Mayers, 31-year-olds Vesa Toskala and Pavel Kubina, and 30-year-olds Boyd Devereaux, Jeff Hamilton, and Tomas Kaberle. It even traded for a 36-year-old Brad May and 33-year-old Martin Gerber at that year's deadline.

With one foot into the rebuild and one foot out, they sputtered to the bottom of the Northeast Division.

THE 2008 DRAFT wasn't the only one Luke attended. While he played out his rookie season in Toronto, Brayden (who was born two calendar years apart from him but just one draft class apart) followed in his footsteps in the WHL to emerge as a top prospect in the 2009 NHL draft with the Brandon Wheat Kings.

After scratching a handful of veterans and recalling some Marlies for the final game of Luke's first season against the Senators in a blatant effort to finish as low in the tightly packed standings as possible, Toronto defeated Ottawa 5–2 to finish the year with 81 points. The win moved them out of a tie in the standings with the Coyotes and Kings, who both finished with 79 points. Had they lost to Ottawa, the Leafs would've lost both tiebreaks to the Coyotes and Kings due to their lower win total of 33. The result? Instead of drafting fifth for the second year in a row, the Leafs' pick slid down to seventh, leaving them with less of a chance at a second Schenn, as Brayden was slotted fourth among North American skaters by NHL Central Scouting.

Still, Luke and Brayden arrived in Montreal for the 2009 draft hoping that they might end up on the same team. On the morning of the draft, the pair ran into Burke at the hotel and the Leafs general manager pulled them aside to tell them they weren't alone in that.

"I hope to have both of you in the Blue and White," he told them.

So when Luke and Brayden arrived at the Bell Centre to take their seats, they both crossed their fingers for another Leafs draft day move-up to select Brayden.

But the uncertainty that had lingered over Luke's day a year earlier hovered over Brayden's too. They knew that John Tavares and Victor Hedman were going to go one-two to the Islanders and Lightning, in that order. But after that, each of the Avalanche, Thrashers, Kings, and Coyotes, who held picks No. 3 through 6, had expressed interest in Brayden and posed a risk to the Leafs' plans. In advance of the draft, the Kings, who selected fifth, had flown general manager Dean Lombardi and some of his scouts into Saskatoon to meet with Brayden in an effort to court him in a way that Luke never had been.

When the Kings made a Schenn the fifth overall pick for the second year in a row by taking Brayden, the Leafs missed on their guy and Luke missed out on playing with his brother. Two picks later, Burke stayed put at No. 7 to draft Nazem Kadri.

"It was just wild the way that it worked out. I still can't believe that because we won that stupid game in Ottawa we slid down to seventh and Brayden ended up going No. 5 to Los Angeles," Luke said.

LUKE NEVER DID become the franchise-altering defenceman he was pedestaled as, but that pursuit was doomed by expectations and circumstance before it was ever allowed to build any momentum. In Luke's second season in Toronto as a 19-year-old, the Leafs again finished last in their division, missing the playoffs for a fifth straight year. In his third, modest improvement pushed them fourth in the division with a 37–34–31 record, which still left them on the outside looking in for a sixth straight year. In his fourth, they bottomed out again, finishing 13th in the Eastern Conference for a seventh and eventually final season outside the playoffs.

Luke never got to be anything but the youngest player on flailing veteran Leafs teams, either. Throughout that fourth season, rumours of a potential trade swirled all year long.

"Hey, this is all just smoke, don't worry about it," Burke told him throughout.

Those rumours never let up, though, and eventually something changed leading into a third memorable draft day for the Schenns.

On Day 1 of the 2012 draft, then Flyers assistant captain Claude Giroux had just finished housing Brayden through his rookie season with the Flyers. (Brayden was traded to Philadelphia in a package for captain Mike Richards.) Giroux had also just played with Luke at the world juniors, and he told Brayden they might get their reunion after all.

"Hey, I think there's a real strong chance he's coming to Philadelphia," Giroux said.

On a group text throughout the evening of the first round, they waited for it to happen. But as the night wound down, they began to question whether it would. Eventually, after a restless night of sleep, Luke's phone lit up with Burke's number. He'd been traded—and it was to Philadelphia after all, a one-for-one trade for forward James van Riemsdyk.

He still remembers the conversation that followed.

"You know, this was a tough deal to make but we had options to trade you to other spots too and if we were going to do it, I wanted you to be able to play with your brother and get to experience that," Burke told him.

He was dealt at 22 years old, still the second-youngest player on that year's Leafs team to defenceman Jake Gardiner. After spending another four seasons in Philadelphia, all with Brayden, Luke was traded to the Kings along with Vincent Lecavalier for prospect Jordan Weal and a third-round pick in 2016. His stint in L.A. began a series of quick pit stops with other teams as he bounced in and out of lineups with the Coyotes, Ducks, and Canucks.

Brayden emerged out of Luke's shadow to surpass him, becoming a 50–70 point player through the prime of his career. In 2019, Brayden won a Stanley Cup as a top forward with the Blues. Luke watched Game 7 of the Final from the crowd, celebrating with his brother on the ice.

"I couldn't have been more proud of him as an older brother and I was just so pumped to see him get his name on that thing," Luke said. "And then for him to have his day with the Cup, it was basically everything I ever wanted to do, and I didn't think I'd ever get the chance to do it getting later on in my career."

Later that summer, after Brayden's day with the Cup, a 29-year-old Luke set out to chase his own day with it in free agency while he still could. When the Lightning called, fresh off a historic season that ended in a stunning first-round sweep to the Blue Jackets, he pounced.

"I knew they'd be coming back hungry with the same core, and I took the opportunity to sign there, thinking I never know how many chances I'm going to get for a team to call," Luke said.

In Tampa, Luke followed his younger brother to make history as one of only a handful of brothers ever to win the Cup in back-to-back years.

That experience has given him a newfound appreciation for everything that led to it, including his four years in Toronto. He says he still has "an unbelievable relationship with Burkie" and keeps in regular contact with the general manager who shipped him out of town.

"Having Burkie unite me with Brayden was pretty surreal," Luke said. "I'll always thank him for that."

He also points to the mentorship he received from Matt Stajan, Mike van Ryn, and Jamal Mayers, among others, as formative—as was all the attention and pressure that came with playing 310 games in the sport's biggest market as a fifth overall pick without a playoff game to show for it. For as scary as his two "welcome to Toronto" moments were, he cherishes those too—especially draft day.

"The whole thing was just a whirlwind and surreal and you can't even believe that you're experiencing it. I was a Leafs fan growing up and to actually get the chance to experience it and wear that uniform and the history that goes along with it, it's pretty special to be a part of it all. I'm grateful for my whole time in Toronto. I wouldn't trade it for anything. The ups and downs and everything that goes along with it, I'd do it all over again," Luke said.

The Islanders turned around and traded all three of the picks they got from the Leafs for Luke *again*. They dealt the seventh overall pick to the Predators, who used the Leafs' pick to draft Colin Wilson, who became a third-line forward in Nashville. They traded the Leafs' 68th pick in the 2008 draft to the Chicago Blackhawks, who took defenceman Shawn Lalonde, who went on to play just one NHL game. And they traded the Leafs' second-round pick in 2009, which became the 37th overall selection, to the Ducks, who got nine NHL games out of defenceman Mat Clark with it.

The Islanders used the picks they got from dealing the Leafs' two 2008 picks to draft Josh Bailey, who became a staple of their franchise for two decades; Aaron Ness, who played 72 NHL games; forward David Ullstrom, who played 49 NHL games for them; and Finn Jyri Niemi, who never made it. A year later, they parlayed the Leafs' 2009 second rounder to move up from 26th overall to 16th overall to draft Nick Leddy, a second staple of their next chapter.

Back on that off-day April call between games with the Lightning, when Luke looks back on the trade that started that ripple effect, the one that was meant to turn him into Toronto's franchise defenceman and set him on his path, he sighs as if he can't believe it.

"When you first come into the league, everyone dreams of winning the Cup, and you're never really sure what your path is going to be. I never would have guessed in a million years what mine would've been, starting in Toronto as a high pick coming in, to all of a sudden fighting to stay in the league and grinding, to going through a few different organizations, to finally getting a crack at a Stanley Cup. It has [taken] a lot of resilience. It was tough to get there," Luke says.

But when he reflects on his draft day and that haze he found himself in, the sigh makes way for a laugh.

"I was actually more nervous for Brayden's draft day than mine. I typically am like that with watching him on TV or him in the Cup Final versus me playing in it. It was crazy how everything kind of worked out. At one point we thought we were both going to end up in Toronto playing together, and it turns out years later we were both in Philadelphia together," Luke says.

Today, he and Brayden spend their summers together in Kelowna, back where his career started with the Rockets, seven doors down from each other in homes on the lake. He now gets to welcome the Davidsons, the billet family who hosted him in their home all those years ago, into his for regular summer barbecues (the Davidsons also visited him at his place in Toronto in that rookie year). His dad, Jeff, has just recently retired from a career in firefighting, and though his parents still technically live in Saskatoon, he guesses that they spend the majority of their time in Kelowna as well.

Between the nearby vineyards, golf courses, hiking trails, time spent on the lake, and the special journey he and his brother have shared, he considers himself only lucky.

"It's crazy the way everything has happened. It has been a roller coaster. But it has all worked itself out in its own way, and I got my name on the Cup because of it," Luke finished. "That's so special for Brayden and I and our family. It's just a little feather in the cap that we were both the same draft pick."

A couple months after we spoke on the phone, Luke Schenn added another feather to his cap.

He won the Stanley Cup with the Lightning. Again.

13

HOW TYLER BIGGS LED TO MORGAN RIELLY AND WILLIAM NYLANDER

THERE IS A danger for teams—in pro sports and in drafting—when what they think will make them successful begins to diverge from the reality of what actually will. And there is a danger for players—in pro sports and in drafting—when teenagers get caught up in that, crushed under the weight of expectations that are either misplaced or unattainable—or worse, both. Life under the microscope can burn when the light is bright. In Toronto, when that light focuses on you, it never lets you step back out of it. And in the history of the Maple Leafs, few have been burned by the weight of expectations and the disconnect of their team more than 2011 first-round pick Tyler Biggs.

Biggs was a tipping point for a Leafs team that thought it knew exactly what it was doing until it diverged far enough away from reality that everything caved in on them, leaving them (and eventually Brendan Shanahan) with no choice but to chart an entirely new course.

So what happened with Biggs and how did his selection get the Leafs back onto a better path at the draft—and, consequently, as an organization? Well, it comes down to a lot more than the words and language—first truculence and belligerence, then bust and failure—that his story became about.

ON A PHONE call a decade after the Leafs infamously traded up to select Biggs 22nd overall in the 2011 NHL draft, Dave Poulin (now a broadcaster with TSN, then a senior member of the Leafs' management group) is still trying to make sense of the layers of things that led to the decision—and eventually to the undoing of a promising young hockey player's career.

He starts with the man in charge, though.

"Hey, Burkie [Leafs general manager Brian Burke] is a factor when Burkie's your boss and you know the kinds of players he likes. And that's still 2011, when Boston had won their Cup with a big, physical group and you were looking at what he could grow into. It was, 'What could Tyler become at 6'3", 220?' And so you were projecting."

There was the outcome, too. Biggs didn't become just a player that the Leafs had drafted too high. He also became a player they'd traded two high picks for. And those two

Left to right at the 2011 NHL Draft: Dave Nonis, Brian Burke, Tyler Biggs, Dave Morrison, and Dave Poulin. *(AP Photo/Andy King)*

high picks had become Rickard Rakell, a two-time 30-goal scorer, and John Gibson, who became one of the league's better starting goaltenders.

"He was hurt immensely because of a couple of players that went after him," Poulin said. "It's such a tough gig. As I think back and reflect over it, it's just such an inexact science it's unbelievable."

Poulin saw things in Biggs that he'd seen in himself in his own playing days, too. He was an undrafted kid who developed a physical, lead-by-example game in college at Notre

Dame and emerged to play 13 years in the NHL, including six as the captain of the Philadelphia Flyers, appearing as an All-Star twice and winning the 1987 Selke Trophy as the league's best defensive forward.

There was also a familial connection that had drawn teams to Biggs through his father, Don. Don was raised in Mississauga, Ontario, and made a name for himself as a hated—and feared—forward with the Oshawa Generals in the OHL. In 1983, the Minnesota North Stars drafted him in the eighth round of the NHL draft. He played nearly two decades in the AHL and IHL before settling in Loveland, Ohio, where he played for the Cincinnati Cyclones, had his number retired, became a member of the AHL Hall of Fame, and raised Tyler.

There was more to it than a general manager who wrongly went after the thing he coveted, too. The Leafs weren't the only team prepared to take Biggs in the first round. In his draft year, Biggs had made a name for himself as the mean, powerful captain of USA Hockey's national development program. The Leafs' scouts were all impressed by how good he'd looked when Team USA had played against college teams and his advanced physicality and athletic maturity had shone through. He'd also just come off an impressive showing at that year's under-18 world championships in Crimmitschau, Germany, leading the Americans to gold (his second under-18 gold, after having played above his age group with Team USA the year prior).

He'd gone through an extensive recruitment process into college, too. You name the school—Notre Dame, Michigan, the rest—and there was interest in Biggs. He ultimately settled on the University of Miami–Ohio because of his local roots and because the team's assistant coach, Chris Bergeron, had played a few years of minor pro with Don.

"The process was the high profile of high-profile schools," Bergeron said.

Bergeron had known Biggs since he was a little kid who'd hang out around the rink, but he began recruiting him heavily in his Minor Midget season as a 15-year-old when he and Don moved to Toronto to play in the GTHL with the Jr. Canadiens in search of stiffer competition for him.

On initial visits to Toronto, Bergeron was blown away by Tyler's play on the ice and how well-spoken and mature he appeared off it.

"He was such a big kid at a young age. He grew quickly and he was almost like a man child really young," Bergeron said.

When Biggs scored 40 goals and 86 points in 72 games to finish seventh in the GTHL in scoring as a 15-year-old, he became such a commodity that Bergeron and the rest of the big college programs who were recruiting him feared he'd go the OHL route as a fast-track to the NHL. But after he went to the national program's 40-man camp and was quickly told he had a place on the team if he wanted it, he accepted and the college path became the choice.

"He was a high-profile young person. He was a really impressive young man who was on this path to the NHL. Having Tyler Biggs commit to Miami at that time was a huge victory for Miami in terms of recruiting," Bergeron said.

While Bergeron was digging into that recruiting battle, he was also pursuing another opportunity for himself to become a head coach at Bowling Green State University. So when he took the job for the 2010–11 season and Biggs showed up that fall for his freshman year at Miami, fresh off being selected by the Leafs in the first round, the coach who'd brought him there was gone.

Rico Blasi, who was then the team's head coach, was still a big believer in Biggs, though, too. And he hoped that the feeling was still mutual.

"In the recruiting process, he was pretty excited to come to Miami. It was him playing at home in front of his family. So everything was great," Blasi said. "He was a really good kid, very polite, worked hard, and then had a pretty decent year at the national team. But once he was drafted in the first round, I think you could see the expectation now that he was going to be what he had dreamt about being all his life."

Biggs didn't have a bad year for a true freshman by any standard, either. Blasi and his staff were actually really pleased with how he played. They used him on the penalty kill and the power play. They went to the national tournament, losing in overtime to end their season. His 17 points in 37 games ranked ninth among all under-19 players in college hockey.

"For me, he was great," Blasi said. "He was a big part of what we were doing that year. He was a good kid, he worked hard, he played a really good role on our team. It was that simple."

But without Bergeron, and without glossy numbers, staff at Miami worried that outside factors and actors had begun to heavily influence where Biggs and the Leafs felt he was at—and consequently, what came next for him.

"I thought he would stay at least two or three years, kind of like some of the players we'd had in the past who ended up making pretty good names for themselves playing in the

NHL or at least earning an opportunity. But I think some of the expectations and pressure that came along with being a first rounder kind of skewed some of his decision-making," Blasi said. "I think that's a real thing that a lot of people don't talk about. Some first-rounders, they get an opportunity to play pro and they kind of get gobbled up in it. I don't think it was all the time that Tyler let himself get wrapped up in it. During the week in practices and games, he was just about playing. But I think maybe in moments where he was watching games, or talking to whoever he was talking to, he felt the pressure of being a first rounder and was constantly thinking, 'Where am I going to be next?' A lot of those guys get caught up trying to be NHLers too fast."

As Biggs tried to navigate all of that, Jeff Twohey, an old opponent of Don's in their OHL days who'd just taken over as general manager of the Generals (the OHL team that owned Biggs' rights after having drafted him back in 2009), called Don to express interest in bringing Tyler to Oshawa, where Don had coincidentally played three years of his own junior career.

When the Leafs committed to an entry level contract if he decided to leave college, Biggs, under pressure from several sides and now the lure of NHL money, decided to leave after his freshman year—"on good terms," according to Blasi—and join the Generals, less than an hour east of Toronto, to play under Twohey and coaches D.J. Smith and Paul McFarland (both of whom coincidentally also went on to coach with the Leafs).

The following season, in Oshawa, the feelings among the Generals staff about Biggs mirrored those of the coaches in

Miami. They liked him. They used him on both special teams and slotted him alongside star Boone Jenner. But when his production continued to fall below expectations, and when it happened in front of Leafs staff like Poulin, Burke, and then director of player development Jim Hughes, who attended most of Biggs' games, the pressure he put on himself—and others placed on him—continued to pile up. As it did, Generals staff began to feel like Biggs, who they knew as a personable kid, had withdrawn himself from his teammates. By playoff time, when he knew he would leave the Generals for the AHL at year's end, they watched as his play, which they also knew to be all-in, began to step out the door. When they lost, and he left, they never heard from him again.

AFTER OSHAWA, BIGGS struggled to find a role with the Marlies and the Marlies struggled with how—and where—to deploy him in their lineup. The rest unravelled quickly, and within a few years he was no longer a member of the Maple Leafs organization. He'd bounced between the AHL and the ECHL and he'd spent half a season in England. By the summer of 2019, at the age of 26, he was out of pro hockey.

All these years removed from Burke's bold draft floor move in Minnesota, those who played a role in Biggs' development feel as if they share in how things went.

Bergeron, who bumped into Don at a game between Miami and Bowling Green a few years back, isn't quite sure where it went wrong, but wishes he'd been there to help guide Biggs through that freshman year.

"I don't know what happened. I just don't know. But it's one of those things that I've been through a couple of times in my career, and I did feel bad that I was the pivot on the recruiting with Tyler and his dad, and then I walk away and it was almost like the guy that drafted you wasn't there anymore," Bergeron said. "And I'm not saying Rico didn't like Tyler's game, because he did, but the relationship that was built between him and Miami, I was the bridge for that and then I wasn't there. And I don't want that to sound selfish because it's not about me, it's about the boy, but you just don't know. When adversity hit, the guy that he had the relationship with wasn't there. Did that have something to do with it? I can't be sure. But when I look back on it, that's something that I wish I would have had a chance to coach that boy."

He also wonders whether, had he been there, Biggs would have stayed for an extra year or two.

"I'm a firm believer that every kid, whether it's first-rounders, seventh-rounders, or free agents, no kid can ever be too prepared. So to me, another year or two in college, you can never go wrong with that," Bergeron said.

When Blasi bumped into Biggs while out for dinner one recent summer, they gave each other a huge hug. He, too, left that interaction wondering what could have been.

"I certainly saw the expectation. I mean, he was 6'3", he had a great shot, he could skate, he had a pretty decent year when he left us, he won a gold medal on the world juniors team, so things were moving in a good direction for him even briefly after he left us. I thought he got better with us, too. Selfishly, as a coach, I would have loved to have had my hands on him for a couple more years just to mature him a little bit, not just his game but emotionally and intellectually like we do with all of our players at the college level," Blasi said, pausing. "But in any event, I thought he was headed in the right direction. I thought he had some upside. Obviously at that point it's up to what he's going to do on a daily basis, and then there's also got to be some luck in terms of the opportunity that comes. I still care about him. He was a part of our family. I think it was just 'I want to get there' and 'I want to see how far I can take this.' And when you're a first-rounder, you've got a lot of different influences that are coming in."

Poulin wonders how things would have been different had the Leafs drafted their other favourites in that slot: Jenner, Brandon Saad, and Vincent Trocheck, all of whom became impactful NHL forwards.

Leafs skating coach Barb Underhill felt that Jenner, after bringing him in for a pre-draft skate, could pick up a step and turn into something. The rest of the Leafs staff had spent a lot of time in Saginaw watching Saad and Trochek, but "both had some baggage coming in" that Biggs didn't, according to Poulin.

"You look back at that draft now and part of the process is considering who you didn't take and why you didn't take them and how personal it is for the scouts that are involved," Poulin said.

Biggs wasn't even the only player he wishes the Leafs got more out of from 2011, either.

Poulin says he's still "baffled" that Stuart Percy, who they took just three slots after Biggs with another first-rounder in 2011, didn't turn into a full-time NHL defencemen. When the Red Wings traded the 24th pick to move back to No. 35, the

Leafs knew that they were doing it because they thought they could get Percy a little further down. Then the Leafs decided to pounce with their No. 25 pick.

"He was such a cerebral player, but he was a quarter of a step slow. And the Red Wings were really high on him because they had a pretty cerebral defenceman there that played the left side who was going to be retiring by the name of Nik Lidstrom," Poulin said, laughing. "Those Detroit guys told me they were comparing his game to Nik. Like that's how smart they thought Percy was. And then he stepped into the NHL and basically played right away, and it was like, 'Oh, jeez, this kid's going to be just fine, he just needs another quarter of a step.' But he never picked up that step."

Poulin can't help but wonder whether things would have turned out differently for Biggs had he not landed in Toronto, too. Both the Washington Capitals (who began the draft with the 26th pick) and the Phoenix Coyotes (who nearly drafted Biggs 20th overall) had been blown away by him throughout the interview process.

The Coyotes were wowed by Biggs in a Team USA game against the University of North Dakota, where the rest of his teammates were completely outmatched and he was the only player who could handle it. They were further impressed at the combine by his fitness levels and the way he spoke, regaling them with his interest in the military.

"Man, that guy's got character," was a common refrain about Biggs among NHL teams during those combine meetings in Toronto in advance of the 2011 draft.

George McPhee, who was then the general manager of the Capitals, told Bergeron that he could count on one hand the number of kids who'd "made an impression on him as a young man as much as Tyler did."

So Bergeron's not surprised the Leafs fell in love with Biggs.

"In the world we live in, we're taking a chance on a human being maybe more than we are the hockey player. And when you're taking a chance on people, those are more calculated risks as far as I'm concerned," Bergeron said.

When he was a recruiter and coach at Notre Dame, Poulin saw firsthand the role environments played in the success of players.

"Kids get in the right environment and just absolutely thrive. And that's up to the team, to create the right environment. And we were doing more and more of that. I was running the Marlies at the time, and the focus was to get the right mix of people. And my last three years with the Marlies, we played nine playoff rounds in three years and lost in the finals. So we were putting the kids in the right environment from that standpoint. But I do think Tyler left college too early, even though I watched him play with Boone Jenner in Oshawa and it was like, 'Oh, this is great,'" Poulin said.

These days, though, none of those what-ifs matter to Biggs anymore. When his hockey career was done, he started over, trained at the Divers Institute of Technology in Seattle, and became a diver for Subsea Global Solutions, a commercial diving company specializing in underwater repairs and maintenance.

But for the Leafs, the effects of his selection lingered long after he was gone. They lingered in the first-round draft pick they used on him and got no NHL games out of, the draft capital they spent to move up to acquire him, and the tarnishing impact both of those things had on how the Leafs brass of the day did business—and scouting.

A year and a half after the Leafs drafted Biggs, Burke was fired. A year and a half after that, Poulin was fired on the same day the Leafs hired 28-year-old Kyle Dubas as their new general manager. Many within the Leafs' scouting department soon followed.

And the organization's path diverged once more, this time in a completely different direction.

IN THE YEARS after the Leafs moved up to draft Biggs, their scouts were directed to look for—and covet—different things. Although the proverbial page didn't flip in an instant (they drafted centre Frederik Gauthier 21st overall for his size and defensive aptitude just two years later), progress began to be made for a team that had for so long struggled to find more than role players in the draft.

That began in earnest at the 2012 draft, when the Leafs, in a greater effort to use their wide-ranging resources, decided to focus on some perceived market inefficiencies. One of them became Sweden and the decision to give the team's most prolific area scout, Thommie Bergman, carte blanche with one pick a year. Those picks became Viktor Loov (a 2012 seventh-rounder who came close to making it before moving to the KHL), Andreas Johnsson (a 2013 seventh-round pick who became a versatile everyday NHL forward), and, in 2014, two more players: would-be star William Nylander, drafted eighth overall, and would-be bottom-six forward Pierre Engvall, drafted 180 picks later. "He basically got the last pick in the draft," Poulin said of Bergman, laughing.

More focus was also placed on spending time scouting overaged players, a decision that produced the 2012 sixth-round selection of late-blooming Erie Otters winger Connor Brown, who went on to become a 20-goal scorer in both Toronto and Ottawa.

But the first big success of the Leafs' new approach and the value it sought to exploit came with their first pick of the 2012 draft in Pittsburgh, when they selected Moose Jaw Warriors defenceman Morgan Rielly with the fifth overall selection. Rielly had just missed almost his entire draft year due to knee surgery but the Leafs, after falling in love with his game at the under-18 world championships, had made sure to do their due diligence.

When the draft rolled around, they knew that his team-mates in Moose Jaw had gravitated toward his personality, even when he was a rookie, and that they'd taken to referring to him as "The Chosen One" for his natural athletic gifts, his advanced physical maturity, and his ability to go end-to-end. They knew, in talking with Dave Hunchak, the Warriors' head coach during Rielly's rookie season (who was replaced for his draft year), that so long as the knee injury didn't linger, Rielly's skating was, as the coach described it, "second to none." They knew, through discussions with long time Warriors general manager Alan Millar, assistant coach Mark O'Leary, and Rielly's billets, the Wattersons, the lengths he'd gone to in his draft year to get back on the ice ahead of schedule during the playoffs, getting back into the gym just days after his surgery. They knew about the regular phone calls he'd make to O'Leary on off-days, and the one time he showed up at the team's hotel in Medicine Hat at 3 AM during the playoffs, when he still wasn't travelling with the team, to support them. And they knew about the long hours he spent in the gym, when the rink was empty, building himself back up, blazing through a rehab unlike any player Millar and his staff had ever seen. Millar insisted in conversations with the Leafs that Rielly was special both on and off the ice. Poulin, who played with Mike Stothers (who took over as Warriors head coach in Rielly's draft year) in Philadelphia, also leaned on that connection while head amateur scout Dave Morrison and his team worked to "look past the injury" in their evaluations and projections.

Late in the draft process, Poulin and Morrison then made the decision to organize family visits with two players. The first was with Russian American centre Alex Galchenyuk, a visit Poulin said went well.

The second was to the Rielly family home in North Vancouver to spend some time with him and meet his parents, Andy and Shirley, and his brother, Connor.

Immediately, Poulin noticed how the socioeconomic background Rielly came from was different from most other elite-level hockey players he'd visited over the years.

"I remember pulling up to some houses while recruiting for Notre Dame or the Leafs and thinking, 'Holy shit, how is this kid going to be motivated to play hockey?' But if you saw Morgan Rielly's house, built into the side of the hill in West Vancouver, you'd be looking over at Mo thinking, 'Oh, boy, you got a totally different experience from that.'"

By the time the meeting was over, Poulin and Morrison both agreed that it cemented him as their guy.

That was further solidified at the scouting combine in Toronto that June, a few weeks before the draft, when the team's interview with one of the draft's other presumptive top picks, Nail Yakupov, went so poorly that, according to multiple people in the meeting, Leafs scout John Lilley "came right over the table" at Yakupov when he answered one of general manager Brian Burke's questions by dismissively blowing and saying, "That's not a question."

"That's the boss; if he asks you a question, that's the question!" Lilley shouted back at Yakupov. "You don't decide what the questions are!"

When the interview was done, Poulin, Morrison, and Leafs scout Garth Malarchuk even took Yakupov out to dinner to say, "Look, that didn't go well," and give him a chance to explain himself, only to come away still feeling uncomfortable about him.

By the time draft day in Pittsburgh arrived, the Leafs had Rielly ranked first on their board.

They also felt they knew what three of the four teams in front of them were going to do, intel that left them confident in the odds that Rielly would be available at No. 5. They believed, as the rest of the hockey world did, that the Oilers would take defenceman Ryan Murray after Kevin Lowe, Edmonton's president of hockey operations and the general manager of that spring's Team Canada, had taken him to the World Championships to preview and get to know him. They knew that the Blue Jackets were likely to follow with Yakupov. And they knew that the Canadiens were partial to Alex Galchenyuk thanks to information from Habs assistant general manager Rick Dudley, who'd left his role as director of player personnel with the Leafs just a month before the draft.

"Rick had worked with us all year and knew our list and had an opportunity to go to Montreal before the draft, and he went on the handshake that he wouldn't be involved in the first round," Poulin said. "And to Dudley's credit, he knew we loved Morgan and there's a reason he's been in the NHL as long as [he has] from a trust standpoint. So I fully assumed, having never had to ask that question, that he wasn't involved in the Galchenyuk pick."

The Islanders, who held the fourth pick in the draft, were, they felt, the only wild card. If they took Rielly, defenceman Hampus Lindholm was going to be the Leafs' guy. But when they drafted defenceman Griffin Reinhart instead, the Leafs felt confident in their due diligence on Rielly, and they didn't hesitate in taking him.

THOUGH THE RIELLY pick was the start of a new chapter for a beleaguered Leafs franchise, it was two years later, after Burke was let go and his lieutenant and replacement, Dave Nonis, was charged with making the team's eighth overall selection in the 2014 NHL draft, that the team's new course was put to the test.

All year long, a player the *old* Leafs would have coveted, 6'2", 226-pound power forward Nick Ritchie—a kid in the Biggs mould who grew up playing for the AAA Toronto Marlies—played just a couple hours north of Toronto in

Peterborough, notching 39 goals, 74 points, and 136 penalty minutes in 61 games for the OHL's Petes.

So in the lead-up to the draft when Ritchie, who disgruntled Leafs fans and media alike expected the Leafs to take right up until the pick was made in Philadelphia and he was still available, wasn't even the Leafs' first, second, third, or fourth option, it sent a clear message internally—and eventually externally when he wasn't their pick—that times were changing.

Bergman, under this new post-Burke leadership, pushed hard for Nylander.

"Thommie felt that William was potentially the most skilled player in that draft. He was on record saying that and we were on record saying that, just from a pure skill standpoint," Poulin said. "And there's a reason he got those late picks. And I don't think anyone expected [Oilers superstar and the third overall pick] Leon Draisaitl to be Leon Draisaitl. No one. No one. No one thought he was going on his way to a Hart Trophy or anything like that."

Others argued on behalf of highly skilled QMJHL import Nikolaj Ehlers. And though the debate came down to Nylander and Ehlers in the end, the Leafs preferred Czech winger Jakub Vrana and Swiss winger Kevin Fiala, all also "skilled kids first," to Ritchie, too. They even circled David Pastrnak, who became one of the draft's top NHL players and was Nylander's close friend and teammate with Södertälje SK in Sweden, as a target if they were to trade back (or trade up to acquire a second first rounder).

They also knew that the way Nylander had bounced around from team to team in his draft year made him harder to scout and raised questions about his motivation for those moves—questions which were heightened by the come-and-go reputation his dad, Michael, had during his own NHL career.

"Michael had played for so many different teams and had had different experiences with different people through those years, and then you also had the Shanahan factor, which came into play there. Shanahan had joined the group and had played with Michael at some point. So you had that in there as well."

The Leafs did their research, only to resolve that the moves had nothing to do with his play or his attitude. (In fact, one of the five moves he made in 2013–14 was to play with his dad in Angelholm with Rogle BK.)

"He was all over the place. I mean, it was crazy. And it was like, 'Is that good, is that bad, what is that?'" Poulin said. "He was in Sodertalje playing with Pastrnak, and then he was in MODO, and then he was back in Sodertalje, and then he was in Rogle."

Coincidentally, two of the places he had spent some time playing hockey were also connections that Poulin shared with him. The first was in Angelholm with Rogle, where Poulin had played before he broke into the NHL. The second was at Notre Dame, Poulin's alma mater. Nylander had skated and trained in the summer at Notre Dame under Andy Slaggert, the team's associate head coach of three decades, and had developed a bond with Slaggert's three hockey-playing kids, Graham, Landon, and Carter.

"Andy kept telling me how great a kid he was, and we just kept coming back to William," Poulin said. "And the allure of Ehlers was he was playing in Halifax, so he had already adjusted to the North American game, but even on that front William is about as North American as you can possibly get after growing up bouncing around the NHL with his dad." The Leafs' bet on Nylander paid off, too. The following season, he exploded in the SHL, spending the first half playing to a point per game with MODO, torching the world juniors, starring for the Marlies in the AHL as a teenager down the stretch, and leaving no doubt about his future NHL potential.

And after years—nay, decades—of blowing the picks that mattered most for all the wrong reasons, the Leafs learned from their Biggs mistake. And now they had Rielly and Nylander, and the skill they needed to build upon for their next, decidedly different, chapter.

They'd gotten two right.

"[In 2012], we really did have Rielly at the top of that list. And I know Burkie said that at the end of the draft, and Burkie's Burkie, but that was the truth," Poulin said. "[And in 2014], it really did come down to William and Nikolaj and the skill. And you know what, you might still have the argument [about Nylander and Ehlers] today, but us having the debate between those two guys was a good sign. It was progress."

14

INSIDE THE 2016
DRAFT LOTTERY WITH
BRENDAN SHANAHAN

STANDING INSIDE SPORTSNET'S studios, Brendan
Shanahan's mind races in the split seconds before deputy
NHL commissioner Bill Daly flips each of the cards that will
determine the future of his franchise.

It's April 30, 2016, almost exactly two years after his hiring
as Maple Leafs president and just three weeks after the conclusion of his second season, and Shanahan is already attending
the NHL Draft Lottery for a second time.

This one feels different than the first one, though.

A year ago, he was ushered into a back room to observe
the drawing of the lottery balls himself. This year, he and
the other team representatives gathered at the Canadian
Broadcasting Centre on Front Street in Toronto's downtown

core were asked to stand on set, with no knowledge of who had won or lost, to learn their fate as the national TV audience did. A year ago, his Leafs had finished his first full season at the helm with 68 points and the fourth-worst record in the league, positioning them with just a 9.5 percent chance to win a lone lottery for the first overall pick in the 2015 NHL draft. So when they didn't win, even after infamously entering the drawing of the fourth and final ball with the best odds (after balls 5, 14, and 6 were drawn, the Leafs held four of the remaining 11 winning combinations to the Sabres' three, the Oilers' two, and the Hurricanes' and Blue Jackets' one apiece), it didn't sting when they stayed put and eventually drafted Mitch Marner, their target after the big two of Connor McDavid and Jack Eichel were gone.

Now, though, the stakes are higher. They're higher because the lottery has changed, replacing a single draw for the first overall pick with one for each of the first three. They're higher because Shanahan's Leafs have just finished with the league's worst record, giving themselves a combined 52.5 percent chance at winning one of the three lotteries (which breaks down to 20 percent at first, 17.5 percent at second, and 15 percent at third), and guaranteeing a pick no lower than fourth. They're higher because even though he'd promised a rebuild, Shanahan knows that he can only show up to the lottery in good faith so many times, and every appearance without a win heightens the pressure on the next. And they're higher because he's representing the Leafs and the five decades of accumulating baggage that comes with them.

As Daly begins to turn over the cards, revealing the draft's order in a countdown from the 14th pick, Shanahan checks

Brendan Shanahan pictured with Leafs draft history, as decided by ping pong balls. *(Graig Abel/NHLI via Getty Images)*

mental boxes in his head, crossing each team off the league's standings, which he has imprinted on his memory.

As each card flips, the crowd of team representatives who surround him begins to shrink and the same word flashes through his brain.

14. Boston Bruins

Good.

13. Carolina Hurricanes

Good.

12. Ottawa Senators

Good.

11. New Jersey Devils

Good.

10. Colorado Avalanche

Good.

9. Montreal Canadiens

Good.

8. Buffalo Sabres

Good.

7. Arizona Coyotes

Good.

Then there's a ripple for the first time and his heart skips a beat as the Flames logo is revealed for the sixth overall pick, meaning the Winnipeg Jets, who hold the sixth-best odds, are among one of the three winners—and the Flames are the first team to fall a spot.

Then there's another ripple in quick succession at fifth overall. It's the Canucks, who held the third-best odds, so the Blue Jackets, whose turn it was supposed to be, have won a second of the three lotteries.

Knowing that just the Leafs and the Oilers remain for the final spot inside the top three, Shanahan's heart rate picks up and his mind races in the brief seconds that follow before the No. 4 pick is revealed.

Be Edmonton. Be Edmonton, he thinks to himself. *Just be in the top three.*

When it's the Oilers logo that lifts off the small podium in front of Daly, he allows himself to smile, feeling as though a spot inside the top three is a victory. But as the broadcast cuts to commercial break, and he stands alone on the set with Blue Jackets president John Davidson and Jets general manager Kevin Cheveldayoff, his brief thoughts of *fair play* and *oh, thank god, we're gonna get a good player* disappear in an instant, replaced by something else.

In the two minutes that pass before cameras begin to roll again, his optimism makes way for the same four words, repeated over and over in his head.

I want to win. I want to win. I want to win, he thinks to himself. *I want the first pick. We deserve something good to happen to this organization. I don't want second, I want to win.*

Then, as they return from commercial, the moment of truth arrives, and Daly is back at the podium to announce the order of the top three.

"The No. 3 overall selection in the 2016 NHL draft belongs to…the Columbus Blue Jackets," Daly says, flipping another white card.

As he does, the camera quickly cuts away to Shanahan, Davidson, and Cheveldayoff. Davidson turns to the other two, extending his hand to shake theirs before exiting the shot.

Shanahan turns back to Cheveldayoff, cracking from his cold exterior to flash a bit of a smirk before adjusting his suit and placing his hands in front of himself, knowing that he's being watched by the camera—and the hockey world.

Out of sight and off camera, the voice of studio host Darren Millard speaks out as suspenseful music is piped into the studio and the broadcast.

"That leaves Winnipeg and Toronto," Millard says, as the shot of Shanahan and Cheveldayoff splits into a double frame shared with Daly.

Stuck in a trance in his place, Shanahan's mind continues to race with different ways of thinking the same thing. *I don't want No. 2. I want No. 1. We need something to fall our way. It's been a long time since something really fell correctly.*

In the time between when Daly turns over the Blue Jackets logo for third overall and he reveals the team that will pick first, skipping over the second pick as an order of process and television theatrics, just 40 seconds pass.

To Shanahan, though, it feels like an eternity.

Finally, Millard hands things over to Daly one last time.

As the words leave his mouth announcing that "the first overall selection in the 2016 NHL draft belongs to…the Toronto Maple Leafs," Shanahan cracks a bigger smile than the smirk he'd let sneak through seconds earlier, coming just shy of revealing his teeth.

Cheveldayoff turns to him and shakes his hand for a second time in congratulations.

One final thought comes over him.

Holy shit, we won.

A LITTLE MORE than five years after that night, Shanahan is driving from his Toronto-area home to pick up some plants during a summer day of gardening when he pauses in the parking lot outside the nursery to sit in his car and re-live the moments that led to the Leafs selecting first overall for just the second time in franchise history.

The memories are all ingrained in him.

He remembers that moment where it was down to the Oilers or the Leafs for the third lottery spot.

"We were standing there and I'm thinking, 'I've seen this before with other organizations where three teams have jumped ahead of them,' and so when Edmonton's card flipped up, there was just this rush of relief that led to that smirk. And at the time Edmonton just kept winning these things. But truly, up to that point I was trying to be very even keeled," he says.

He remembers that final flipped card, describing how those last "10 or 15 seconds felt like 10 or 15 hours" until he finally let out that smile.

"For people that know me well, everyone was like, 'You were trying to stifle the smile and then you couldn't hold it back anymore,'" he says, laughing.

He even remembers the process that led to the Leafs deciding they would use their card in the lottery to reveal their new logo for the first time.

"It was like, turn over a new leaf," he says.

After his "holy shit" moment, he remembers thinking of all the diehard Leafs fans who were sitting at home feeling the same way he was, and the vote of confidence those fans had given him when he'd laid out his plan for what amounted to tanking (though he won't go as far as using that word).

"What I was really impressed with was the support that we got from the fan base to do a proper build. There was always this reason why people heard you couldn't do it in Toronto was because the fans would never allow for it. And I felt just the opposite when we stated we were going to do it," Shanahan says.

He credits those fans for the way they followed the Leafs' prospects and the Marlies during those years too, because he knows that the NHL club was suffering.

"What is a little bit unique about playing in a Canadian city or in a really good hockey market is even over the next couple of years after the lottery win, even though these guys weren't necessarily playing in the NHL, our fans started to recognize the prospects that were in the system. I think in some non-hockey markets you only recognize the people that are playing on your team but what helped us was the knowledge of our fans that were seeing some of these prospects that were 18, 19 years old and had tremendous upside," Shanahan says.

But he also remembers just how hard those first two years were, and how easy it would have been to bail on the blueprint he'd laid out for the organization when he was first hired back on April 11, 2014.

"It was difficult because you are clearly and publicly in a state of rebuild where you are trying to acquire draft picks, but you are also still trying to establish a certain culture. And the two in some ways sometimes conflict with one another, so it's a difficult balance. And as much as I felt it was something that we had to do and we look back now and say, 'Oh, it was a couple of years of picking fourth overall and first overall, boo hoo,' those are long nights. Those are long nights…" he says, trailing off. "It doesn't seem like a short amount of time when you're in it. We never as an organization wavered from what we said we were going to do, but I would say to any organization that's about to go through it, that it's the right thing to do in certain circumstances but it's not easy. There were some real difficult nights where we played against teams that were just better than us."

While he knew that night that Auston Matthews was their guy, the Leafs didn't admit as much on air to honour the commitment they'd made amongst each other within the organization to spend the May and June that followed making sure that when the draft came, they had no doubts that he was the best player and pick in the class.

"You owe it to yourselves and the organization and everyone to go through the entire process once you know exactly where you're picking. And picking first overall is a unique situation because you truly are in control. Every other draft, no matter where you're drafting, to a certain degree the teams before you may dictate who you take or don't take. This one was so unique in that it was really up to us," Shanahan said. "We felt quite strongly that night that it was going to be Auston and then in the coming weeks as we did our due diligence, nothing changed. But we kept that to ourselves until Mark Hunter said his name on the stage."

Though Shanahan never had to sit through a draft lottery to see who would pick him because that process wasn't created in earnest until 1995, eight years after he was chosen second overall by the New Jersey Devils in the 1987 NHL draft (before the lottery, the reverse order of the standings guaranteed a team's pick), he has tried in the years since to relate to Matthews through their shared experiences as top picks and eventually star players.

"It's something that we do for all of our players but certainly I think when you're a star player of a team, there are expectations and players put expectations on themselves. But if you're going first overall, you don't get drafted and then say, 'Oh, expectations? That's new. Pressure? That's new.' Guys like

Left to right on stage for the Leafs' historic 2016 draft moment: Lou Lamoriello, Auston Matthews, Mark Hunter, and Mike Babcock. *(Nathan Denette/The Canadian Press via AP)*

Wendel, guys like Auston, they've been dealing with pressure and expectations since they were little kids. But I think that any organization has to really believe that no matter where you stack up in the league or where you stack up in a team's lineup, you help players, and you help them fulfill and meet or exceed their potential. And you try to give people all the support you can, so that they can have all of the success that they can. That goes for not just guys who go first overall, but for everyone."

Shanahan also acknowledges that any number of things could have led the Leafs down a different path. Had they won just one more game that season, he points out that they would have leap-frogged the Oilers to finish 29th in the standings, and an identical drawing of the balls would have given Edmonton Connor McDavid *and* Auston Matthews for their fifth lottery win in seven years and the Leafs the fourth overall pick (which the Oilers used on Jesse Puljujarvi) for the second year in a row.

"When you're in that position, you need a little luck to fall your way," he said.

As for the lottery and the role it plays in determining that good and bad luck for teams? Shanahan says he has never been a strong proponent or opponent one way or the other in its designs.

"I don't have a strong opinion on some of the tweaks that they've made to it. But the general concept that there is a lottery, and that even if you finish in last place there's no guarantee that you draft first, I think is a fair one," he said. "We went into that lottery with an 80 percent chance of not getting the first pick even though we finished in dead last. So

I think there's a certain integrity and fairness in that it's not guaranteed. I don't mind the draft lottery at all."

Above all else, though, he acknowledges that the job didn't end with that lottery win and Matthews. He knows that winning a Stanley Cup comes down to much more than that. But the two years that led to Matthews were a necessary means to an end, nonetheless.

"As much as you just wanted to figure out a way to win right away, we knew we probably needed to go the opposite direction for a little bit in order to come out the other end. And we're still in that process," Shanahan said.

Those two years also taught Shanahan and his staff that patience will pay off in that process. When failure followed at various points in the form of first-round defeats in 2017, 2018, 2019, 2020, 2021, and 2022, their lessons learned from time spent at the bottom helped them stick with their pursuit of the top.

"Our view was that if we had the patience and did this the right way with some trades, some free agents, player development, but most importantly and at the heart of it, find a way to draft core pieces—which we did at fourth overall and first overall—and build around them, then we could build something that was sustainable for a long period of time," Shanahan finished. "That was, and still is, our goal. It's even more relevant today than it was back when we planned the build. I believe in them."

15

JACK HAN AND THE CROSSROADS BETWEEN DRAFTING AND DEVELOPING

WHEN YOUNG PEOPLE reach out to Jack Han with questions about how he broke into the hockey world, or for advice on how *they* can, they typically have their sights set on one of two jobs—that of a scout or that of a player development coach.

His advice usually surprises them.

"If you're looking to become a good scout, become a better player development coach. And at the same time, if you want to be a better player development coach, then learn how to be a better scout too because then you'll learn to really observe and really have a mental model of what you look for in a player and how to build a profile in a player," he'll tell them. "Those are two things that I think really feed into each other. Even now, most teams have those two things separate, where your scouts and your player development guys don't really talk to each other all that much. For me, having that two-way conversation is essential because you're constantly handing players off to one another."

There are few in hockey who have worked to bridge the gap between scouting and player development quite like Han has. And even fewer are more intimately familiar with how the Leafs are trying to merge the two than he is.

From August 2017 to May 2020, he worked in three different jobs within the Leafs organization. While his title changed, going from Leafs player development analyst to Leafs hockey operations assistant and then Marlies assistant coach, the job was always the same—he was the go-between for Leafs assistant-general-manager-turned-general-manager Kyle Dubas, his player development department, and his scouting department.

It was a job that was originally created by Dubas specifically for him. And it was a period of time in Leafs history that saw the organization throw out the old in favour of the new, beginning with Brendan Shanahan's "scorched-earth" organizational overhaul, which was marked by the replacement of much of the staff he inherited and included new voices like Dubas' and eventually Han's.

In the summer of 2021, a year removed from his decision to leave the Leafs organization on his own terms, Han paused during a trip to California to visit his parents to reflect on his time with the Leafs and offer rare insight into the inner workings of the organization from the draft to the NHL.

"WHAT DO YOU think of analytics?"

That was the first question that Lou Lamoriello asked Han in his job interview. Han was seated in a conference room at 8:30 AM on a summer day in 2017 interviewing for a role that the Leafs were calling "player development analyst." There were two people seated across the table from him. There was Lamoriello, then the team's general manager, and there was Dubas, then the team's assistant general manager. He knew Dubas reasonably well by then. In January of that year, Dubas had begun following Han (then an analyst with McGill University's women's hockey team who had begun to also do some of his work publicly) on Twitter and had reached out a couple of times to pick his brain on different topics. That March, after a heartbreaking double overtime loss in the final at nationals to the University of Alberta, and a night of drinking and goodbyes with the Martlets (who'd outshot the Golden Bears by a margin of two-to-one only to lose off of a shin pad deflection, Han will tell you), it was Dubas who'd texted a hungover Han while he was on the bus back to Montreal to say that he'd like to speak with him in more detail about a role he had in mind for him with the Leafs. After playing phone tag with their availabilities and a couple months of radio silence, it was also Dubas who, shortly after the 2017 NHL draft and the Leafs development camp that followed, finally got back in touch to say, "OK, let's get you a flight booked, I'd like to bring you in for an in-person interview."

But Han and Lamoriello had never met, or even spoken, before they were introduced in that room. Han didn't know that Lamoriello would be a part of the interview either, because Dubas had given him no indication that he would be.

But Han was familiar with Lamoriello. He was familiar with Lamoriello the hockey man, the mystique that he had created about himself, and the way he ran his teams, because he'd gone to middle school in New Jersey and had grown up watching the Devils teams that Lamoriello built. But he was also familiar with something else about Lamoriello—that once upon a time, Lamoriello was a high school math teacher. He knew that because before he'd left for Toronto, longtime hockey journalist and family friend Michael Farber had told him as much.

"You know, if you ever meet Lou, he has this reputation of being very traditional, of being very anti-analytics, but he was actually a high school math teacher and he's really way more of a numbers guy than you think," Farber told him.

"Hmm, that's interesting," Han replied, tucking away that information.

So, when Lamoriello sat through the first few minutes of Han's job interview in complete silence, and then delivered what Han describes as a "point-blank, very vague, loaded question" from a "very cagey guy," he knew how to answer it.

He launched into an answer about calculus.

"Calculus," he said, "is a way for you to decode what a curve's properties are."

In a hockey application, he explained, calculus can be applied in a few ways. One, he said, was in mapping out player aging curves.

"You start out, you're 16, 17, 18, you're in juniors, you're quickly improving, you hit your early twenties, that's probably your early peak, and then you hit your late peak around 25–27, maybe a little bit later, and then after 30 you're declining," he explained. "And every player has an aging curve, and every age curve looks broadly the same—*but* then there's a lot of variation among individuals."

Another, he said, was in measuring things like their Wins Above Replacement (or WAR) relative to their aging curve.

"So if Connor McDavid is 20 years old right now, we can expect his curve to go up. There's a certain shape to it. Then, if you look at the first derivative of the curve, you get a trend," Han said. "And that is essentially analytics because you create a model, you put in a player's past results, and then you get an estimate of his future outputs and you can fit that player's future results on a curve. That's what we're looking to do—we're looking at your past performance compared to your immediate peers and then we're trying to predict what you're going to do in the future. Which is a pretty neat way to do things. And I think there's a lot of value in that."

And then before he finished and left Lamoriello to comment on his answer, he paused and said one last thing.

"But I also believe that that outlook is incomplete because what you need to care about is not only what your value is right now and what your future outlook is, but you're also looking to *influence* what your future outlook is. So, are you eating well, are you sleeping well, are you making technical changes, are you expanding your game tactically? And that's the second derivative," Han continued. "And as an organization, as a coach, and as a player, you're able to influence that day-in and day-out. And there's a reason why we always have a margin of error when we talk about a player's future outputs because we don't know what's going to happen. Maybe injuries flare up, maybe he trains a different way, maybe he finds a new skills coach, maybe the family situation changes, maybe he's just not happy. But that second derivative, we're able to influence and for me, that's what I want to learn more about. That's something that I feel is really important in a way that maybe isn't captured in just looking at an aging curve or WAR."

When Han was finally done, Lamoriello sat back in his chair for a moment, just kind of stared at him, and then spoke from the awkward silence.

"That's a perfect answer," he said.

WHEN HAN GOT the job, he knew that his answer to Lamoriello's question likely helped seal the deal.

He also knew that both the time was right and the Leafs were the right fit. The time was right because he'd decided heading into the 2016–17 season at McGill that his third year with the program (which also coincided with the departure of the team's star, Melodie Daoust) would be his last, he had prepared to pass off his role to his successor, and he wanted to go all-in on breaking into pro hockey in analytics, scouting, or coaching. He knew that the Leafs were the right fit for him because he felt like he could help them in their pursuit of a holistic top-down organization where every department was on the same page. He'd told himself that he would pick his own boss; he'd followed Dubas' ascension closely enough that he knew he was different (a word he also uses to describe himself); and he felt that if they had the chance to work together that he would jump on it.

For much of his first season with the Leafs, Han spent his time watching the team's drafted prospects, breaking down their shifts, tracking and collecting data on them, quantifying their progress, discussing it with player development leads Scott Pellerin and Stephane Robidas, and getting on the ice with player development consultant Darryl Belfry to serve as his video assistant, filming the prospects' skates on an iPad.

In March of that season, Dubas then began to send Han names of players he was interested in for the 2018 NHL draft so that he could track their games, send him findings from the data, break down the tape, and provide his opinion on their stylistic fit for the organization. When he was done with one batch of four or five names in one week, another followed at the start of the next. The lists themselves were diverse, ranging from top-10 prospects to second-round targets, late-round picks, and undrafted overagers.

"I really got a mix of everything and then I just kind of went about it with the same process I used for our drafted players. And the process itself was something that I came up with on the fly because I was in a new role, so I actually had a lot of freedom and I just went off what I was doing at McGill in terms of the video and the analytics pieces and I evolved it a little bit. So by the time the draft rolled around,

I actually became really familiar with a lot of the players that were going to be in our wheelhouse."

The idea itself, which Han believes Dubas took from a leaked presentation that former Canucks general manager Mike Gillis gave to the Penguins, was Dubas' way of getting a second opinion on some of the players independent of the team's scouts. It was also, Han believes, part of some behind-the-scenes maneuvering that was happening at the time between Dubas and fellow assistant general manager Mark Hunter (who Dubas knew was viewed as a super scout of sorts) to position himself as the heir apparent to Lamoriello.

"[Gillis] talked about having two different scouting teams go head-to-head and that was what we did that spring and summer, basically," Han said. "It was just me and Kyle doing our own homework on these guys so that he had his own book."

During that process, one player in particular left a "really strong impression" on Han—overager Joey Keane of the Barrie Colts, who'd posted 44 points in 62 games in the OHL that season. Across a five-game segment of evaluation, which included watching all of Barrie's shifts instead of just Keane's, Han found that when Keane wasn't on the ice, every single transitional metric suffered, from controlled exits and entries, to exits and entries against, to shots for and against.

"He just had this dominant effect at tilting the ice for Barrie," Han said. "Even though his point totals weren't huge, I just thought that this was the kind of player that statistically would project really well because he was able to be dominant at 5-on-5. And this was a guy who'd went undrafted and would possibly be available in the third, fourth, or fifth round and beyond. I really thought that this guy would be someone who would play the way that Kyle envisions but also just be someone who brings value in a whole spectrum of areas."

By the time the Leafs' pre-draft combine rolled around, and they'd welcomed a couple dozen players to Toronto (including Keane, would-be third-round Leafs draft pick Semyon Der-Arguchintsev, would-be Predators fifth-rounder Spencer Stastney, and future Leafs signee Pavel Gogolev), Han decided to put his affinity for Keane to the test by approaching Belfry to ask him to identify the player at camp that he liked the most without knowing who that player was.

"OK, there's one kid here who I think will be a really good NHL prospect for us. I would like for you to guess who that player is," he told Belfry on the morning of the combine, before one of his skates.

"Alright, I'll keep an eye out," Belfry answered.

Midway through the session, Han skated over to Belfry.

"OK, so the guy that I'm thinking of, do you have an idea of who that might be?" he asked.

"Spencer Stastney," he said, pointing at him with his stick.

"No, take a second guess," Han answered.

"This guy's skating is projectible," Belfry answered quickly, pointing at Keane.

Though the Leafs never ended up picking Keane, who was drafted 88th overall by the Rangers that June (12 picks after the Leafs selected Der-Arguchintsev) and has since played two games for the Hurricanes, who traded for him, in the NHL, that experience allowed Han to trust his instincts.

"In my mind, if I've already identified this player and Darryl's also able to identify him quickly, then we've really got something because that's where the quantitative and the qualitative side really come together, and we could be really confident taking a chance on this player. At that moment, when Darryl pointed him out second, I really thought if we could somehow sneak this guy into one of the later rounds that we would really have something," Han said.

FOLLOWING THE MARLIES' Calder Cup championship at the end of Han's first season with the organization, and Dubas' promotion to general manager on May 11, 2018, Han's three-pronged role within the team began to evolve into the 2018–19 campaign.

After the 2018 NHL draft in Dallas, that expanded role included a more hands-on involvement in the development of the Leafs' prospects through that off-season's summer camps and into a new Marlies season in the fall.

One of the first players he left his mark on was 2014 seventh-round draft pick Pierre Engvall, who'd come to Toronto via a season with HV71 in the SHL late in the Calder Cup push and was just beginning his first full season in North America.

After breaking down a great deal of Engvall's tape before he arrived with the Marlies and then watching him throughout the Calder Cup playoffs, Han concluded what nobody else within the Leafs organization had yet tabled: "We should try Engvall as a centre."

He came to that conclusion after having read voraciously about Pete Mahovlich while growing up in Montreal.

"I had never seen Pete play…he was a winger growing up but he got moved over to centre because he was a big guy, he was like 6'5" like Pierre, and he skated really well, like Pierre, and he had a really good ability to protect the puck, like Pierre. So he went from a decent left-wing prospect, he got moved over to centre, and he ended up being probably the most productive centre who played with Guy Lafleur and Steve Shutt. So I was like, 'Hmm, Pierre looks like what I figure Pete Mahovlich was and we don't have any centres who are close to ready; we don't have any high-end centre prospects, so that could be interesting,'" Han said.

After reviewing some more of Engvall's game, Han then went to Marlies head coach Sheldon Keefe with the idea in October of the 2018–19 season.

Initially, Keefe was resistant, in large part because whenever Engvall had taken draws as a winger, he'd been terrible at them.

Eventually, with some prodding and consideration, Keefe then began to turn to Engvall as a centre every once in a while, after a penalty kill or for the odd neutral-zone faceoff.

"He would just tell Pierre, 'OK, I'm going to send you out with two wingers, you just go play centre for a bit,'" Han said of the decision to give him the odd shift down the middle.

Han remained insistent that they give him a longer look, though. At the midway point of that season, a whole slew of things eventually came together to allow that to happen when the Marlies lost centres Sam Gagner (to a recall by the Canucks) and Chris Mueller (to injury).

"We essentially had like Adam Brooks and then nobody," Han said of the way things played out. "So I just I kept alluding to it or bringing it up to [Keefe]. And he was smart about it. He kind of eased him in that way."

The move proved pivotal for the 2018–19 Marlies, and for Engvall's development, eventually giving a Leafs organization short on centre depth beyond Auston Matthews and John Tavares a versatile depth option. A year after he made the move to the middle, Engvall was recalled by the Leafs and quickly signed to a two-year contract extension when he was successful.

IN ADVANCE OF Han's second draft as a member of the Leafs organization in 2019, and under Dubas' guidance as general manager for the first time, Han was invited to Buffalo for the league's scouting combine and then Vancouver for the draft itself so that he could factor into some of the team's new processes for decision making.

One of those new processes was, for the very first time, the Leafs' attempt to test the functional intelligence of the players who were at the combine.

The goal was to try to evaluate their hockey sense and learning ability. The plan—after discussions between Han, Dubas, Dr. Meg Popovic (who had been hired in August of the year prior as the team's director of athlete well-being), and other members of the Leafs' development staff—was to get Han in the room at the combine with his laptop, show the players clips of the Leafs and the Marlies, and then ask them what they see coming or would have done on a given play.

Two days before the combine, Leafs skills coach Adam Nicholas, who also worked with the Chicago Steel, then reached out to Han when he noticed that Steel overager Nick Abruzzese was on their combine interview list.

"You're really going to love this guy, he's really going to blow your socks off from a hockey sense point of view and from an intelligence point of view," Nicholas told Han.

In the lead-up to the combine, Han then went out of his way to do some video analysis of Abruzzese, a double overager who was committed to Harvard, to see it for himself, only to come to the same preliminary conclusion about Abruzzese's smarts.

On the day of the combine, he also kept in mind a common adage of Belfry's—"If you have a player that's special or elite, you've got to find a way to stretch him; you've got to find a way for him to show you something new and force him to elevate."

By the time it was Abruzzese's turn, Han found himself thinking two things.

The first was, *Well I'm expecting a lot out of Nick Abruzzese.*

The second was, *I'm looking for a lot because he's going to have to override his poor results earlier on. And for him to be even a possible NHL player, he's really going to have to outperform his statistical profile to date and he's really got to show me a lot of projectible traits.*

After going through one process with the first several players the Leafs had interviewed that day, Han then decided to flip the script on Abruzzese and make his job a little harder.

After the usual process had played out and the floor was left to Han to question Abruzzese, he told him that every other player had been given the opportunity to watch a series of clips once and then on their second time through they were allowed to tell him to pause whenever they had an observation, but that he would not get that opportunity.

Instead, Han told Abruzzese that he was only going to play the clip once, that Han was going to have control of when to stop the clip, and that whenever he did, he wanted Abruzzese to predict what was going to happen next, whether that was where the puck was going, who was going to get it, whether it was going to be a shot or a pass, or how the defenceman was going to react.

"They got a very open-ended question," Han said. "I was basically asking him to predict the future. That's how I wanted him to elevate. So he doesn't know the players, he doesn't know the system, he doesn't know the opponents. I'm really just looking to test his crystal ball and see how good it is."

In the first clip Han began playing, the first unit of the Marlies power play was coming up the right flank when Han hit pause almost immediately.

Abruzzese didn't hesitate with his analysis, jumping right into it.

"Number 27, that's Jeremy Bracco and knowing Bracco, he's probably going to go for a seam pass," Abruzzese said.

When Han pressed play, Bracco attacked downhill and hit a seam pass.

A few seconds later in the same clip, when Han paused it again, Abruzzese called the play a second time.

And a few seconds later, he did it again.

"He was spot-on every single time. I stopped it three times and all three times he was able to predict where the puck was going," Han said. "So right away, that for me shows that in terms of hockey sense, he was going to be elite. That's a hard thing to identify if you don't know what you're looking for or how to tease it out, but that exercise was what we felt was the simplest way, and the most impressive player in that exercise was Nick Abruzzese."

A month later, the Leafs selected Abruzzese in the fourth round of the 2019 NHL draft. A season later, Abruzzese posted 44 points in 31 games as a freshman at Harvard and won the ECAC's Rookie of the Year award as college hockey's third-highest-scoring player. Two years after that, the Crimson named him team captain, he played for Team USA at the Olympics, and the Leafs signed him.

AFTER HIS PROMOTION to Marlies assistant coach in the summer of 2019, Han spent one last season within the Leafs organization until he decided in May 2020, at the age of 31, to step away from the team, return to work in the public sphere (which included authoring a series of books on hockey tactics), and pursue other opportunities.

The decision to leave was one he didn't take lightly, but he felt was necessary as one chapter of the Marlies closed and another opened following the promotions of Dubas, Keefe, and others.

"Imagine you're driving on a two-lane highway where there's only one lane going in each direction, and then you come up on a car that you want to pass. What do you do?" Han said. "Well, if you want to pass that car, either you've got to change lanes and make the pass and take some risk while you're doing that, or you wait behind that car until that car turns off. Those are the only two ways that you're going to get past that car that's blocking you. And whichever choice you make is fine, but you've got to make a choice and commit to that."

Today, though, he looks back on his three years with the Leafs organization with pride for what he contributed at the crossroads between several departments, and gratitude for the opportunity Dubas gave him to help a team toward that Calder Cup in 2018. When he talks about what he saw in Keane, or the role he played with Engvall, or that combine interview process with Abruzzese, he speaks assuredly about the impact he had in both scouting and helping to develop not only the kids but the organizational processes and data that helped to study and support them.

"There's a mix of quantitative analysis and qualitative analysis that goes into it for the kids. I think the three years that I was there, we were able to build on that. And that was kind of the lens through which I did everything. Certainly, there's the numbers way of doing it and saying, 'Does this player's past production project well to this league?' So that's the quantitative way. The qualitative way is looking at the players' technical and tactical and physical skill sets and saying, 'Does this translate?' So does the player use a lot of outside speed to beat defenders, because that's less projectible than a player who plays between checks, who uses deception, who turns defenders' feet," Han said. "And once you get familiar with a player's profile on both sides of the fence, then you can start having a much better idea of, first of all, 'How does this guy project?' and second of all, 'How can we influence his game on a day-to-day or month-to-month basis so that he has the best chance to either hit his projection or outperform his projection?'"

He often wonders how things might have turned out differently for him, and for the Leafs for that matter, had Dubas left the Leafs in 2017 for a job with the Avalanche (which the Leafs had allowed him to pursue while he was assistant general manager). He knows, surely, that he never would have interviewed for his job with the Leafs, and he never would have answered that question from Lamoriello.

But the very best thing that happened to him from 2017 to 2020, as the Leafs tried to go about building their team differently than they had in the past, was the same thing he tells all the people who reach out looking for advice.

"I didn't go into that job expecting to learn a lot about scouting or even to learn that much about player development to be honest. I expected it to be more of a stats-driven job. But ultimately what I was really happy about was that I became a pretty good scout because I became a much better player development coach," Han finished. "I already had a pretty decent understanding of the stats side of things, and projecting, and league equivalencies, and microstats going in. But once I got there, I got to learn about what to look for in the skater, or what to do to make a player skate better, or stickhandle better, or protect the puck better, or pass the puck better. And that really gave me a whole appreciation of what kind of players, even in the same points-per-game range or the same age-adjusted production range, are more projectible than others."

16

THE PANDEMIC
DRAFT KID

THERE AREN'T MANY "Where were you when?" moments
in life that we all share—that we can all pinpoint to a
certain place and time. But sports have a way of manifesting
those moments. In hockey, how many people say they were
there, or will tell you where they were, the night Darryl Sittler
scored 10 points, the day Wayne Gretzky was traded, or the
afternoon Sidney Crosby's golden goal slid underneath Ryan
Miller? I wasn't alive for those first two moments, but I can tell
you where I was for the last one—in a bar in Florida with my
parents, on our way to visit my aunt Jane, on my 15th birthday.
I remember because we had to ask our waiter to change one
of the bar's many televisions to the game while everyone else
was watching the NASCAR race (the 2010 Shelby American)
that was on that day.

There are even fewer days in sports history as unmistakable as March 11, 2020, the day COVID-19 stopped basketball and the NBA stopped the world—or at least our little piece of it in North America. The pandemic didn't start then. The virus had already been spreading for months, getting people sick and worse. But I remember it because a couple weeks earlier, for a different one of my birthdays (my 25th), a group of my friends and family had gotten together to celebrate. On February 28, 2020, we crowded around a table at a Toronto bocce ball bar, and we drank and played, sans masks, with no discussions of the pandemic, or gathering size, or risk. I've often talked with those people about how that night was our last of the Before Times. And if that's true, then March 11 was the first day of the After Times marked by the pandemic. And it all started with a sport, and an athlete, when the Utah Jazz's Rudy Gobert tested positive, and the NBA decided to announce the suspension of its season.

It was the start of the After Times because it was a turning point, an awakening to the power of the virus. A day later, the NHL scrambled to put its season on pause as a reaction to the NBA. Within a week, almost every major hockey league in the world had done the same. And by the end of the month, restrictions and lockdowns had swept across the continent as governments took the NBA's lead (long after doctors and experts had already told them to act).

For the 2020 NHL draft class, the sudden pauses—which eventually became outright cancellations—meant the end of their draft year. Just like that, there were no more games to play, no more opportunities to impress scouts, no more playoffs, no more Memorial Cup (for the first time in its

101-year history to that point, after it had survived being awarded through two World Wars), no more under-18 worlds. Nothing.

For a moment, whether the draft would even take place was drawn into question, with discussions about postponing it a year and combing two draft classes into one for 2021. Eventually, it was moved from Montreal's Bell Centre and its planned June 26–27 dates to October 6–7 at the NHL Network's studios in Secaucus, New Jersey, leaving the players to spend their summers waiting for their name to be called.

And the Leafs, armed with less information about the players than they'd planned for, would make 12 selections, their most since the draft's reduction to seven rounds a decade and a half earlier.

For each of those 12 players, the pandemic played an immeasurable, still-yet-to-be-determined role in not just the way their draft seasons finished or their draft day unfolded (a day which was nothing like the one they'd spent their lives imagining), but also in the season that followed when the tangles of COVID-19 held on for longer than anyone imagined.

Among those 12 draft picks, no player was caught up in it more than Ryan Tverberg, the Leafs' very last pick of the 2020 draft.

THE START OF Ryan Tverberg's story is a lot like most other hockey players' stories. His dad, Todd, was born to Norwegian ancestry but is from Minnesota and grew up playing the sport through high school, making it as far as one season in college at the University of St. Thomas (which is today a Division I program but was then a Division III program) before he quit. Todd met Paddy, an Asian Canadian, in Vegas when he was 29, and when the two got married they moved together to her hometown, the Toronto suburb of Richmond Hill, where they raised three kids. Cayla, their eldest, was born a year (almost to the day) before Ryan, the middle child. Chloe, their youngest, was born six years later. Cayla and Chloe did competitive dance. At two years old, Todd got Ryan into skates. Todd coached Ryan until he was in Tyke (now known as U7, or under-7) before handing over the reins to others so that he didn't become the coach-dad who was always yelling at his kid. After Todd stopped coaching Ryan, he made hockey his full-time job in another way, running tournaments, skates, and camps around the city. Today, Paddy operates Maclaw, an artificial plant company that outfits indoor spaces like airports and hotel chains with fake trees, and Todd operates Prospects by *Sports Illustrated*, running hockey tournaments and camps around North America for top minor hockey, junior and college players.

"It's the same old story," Todd said, laughing, of Ryan's hockey upbringing.

In Atom and Peewee from 9 to 12 years old, Ryan (who played his entire minor hockey career for the AAA Toronto Jr. Canadiens) and eventual Winnipeg Jets first-round pick Cole Perfetti were considered the two most talented players in their age group in the Greater Toronto Area. By Bantam and into Minor Midget, though, as other players began to hit their growth spurts as teenagers, Ryan, who had always been one of the smallest players on his team, never grew, putting him on a different path than his peers. When he finished seventh on the Jr. Canadiens in scoring with 19 points in 33 games in his OHL draft year at 15, he had to wait until the 12th round of the 2018 OHL draft to be selected by the Hamilton Bulldogs—a selection that happened in part because the team's coach at the time, former NHLer John Gruden (who went on to become an assistant coach with the New York Islanders shortly after taking Ryan), was a close friend of Todd's from Minnesota.

Despite a strong first training camp and preseason with the Bulldogs, where Ryan impressed as one of their better 2018 draftees, the combination of his size and where he was picked meant he was never going to make the team as a 16-year-old. After meeting with several Junior A teams later that fall, he decided against playing in the OJHL in favour of returning to minor hockey to play for the Midget AAA Jr. Canadiens in a first-line role (instead of the third- or fourth-line role he'd been promised at the second-tier junior level), a decision that, at the time, turned his focus to a college hockey scholarship and almost surely put the NHL draft out of the question.

"Ever since Ryan was a little kid, I always tried to turn him onto the NCAA way of things, just because of, No. 1, how many people actually really end up making it and it's good for him to have something to fall back on, and No. 2 because I was a little bit of a late bloomer too and now I'm a little over 6'0"," Todd said. "I didn't grow until I was 18. So when Ryan was little and my wife was always giving it to me because all of these other kids were getting bigger, I was always like, 'It's coming, just wait.'"

He was right, too. At 17, after that final year in minor hockey and into an NHL draft year that had previously felt unattainable, Ryan grew, sprouting up to 5'10" (today he's 6'0", just like his dad) and making the jump to the Jr. Canadiens' OJHL team, this time as a first-line player.

From there, his draft year, even before the pandemic hit, was a whirlwind. Out of nowhere, Ryan started his first season at the Junior A level with seven goals and 13 points in 11 games through September and early October, sneaking his way onto NHL Central Scouting's early players to watch list with a "C" rating, indicating him as a potential late-round candidate for the 2020 draft. With the NHL Central Scouting recognition came his first real interest from NHL clubs and top college hockey programs. That fall, 41 college hockey programs reached out and he had to pick which five he was going to visit. (Recruits aren't allowed to visit more than five under the NCAA's bylaws.) After visiting Harvard, UMass, Princeton, Western Michigan, and Cornell, he announced his commitment to Harvard on December 24 of his draft year. And at ScotiaBank Pond, the Jr. Canadiens' home arena in the Toronto neighbourhood of Downsview, the Leafs, in part because of their proximity and in part because of their interest, became Ryan's most recurring guests, attending almost every one of his games. After being ranked 122nd among North American skaters on NHL Central Scouting's January 13 midseason list, he then impressed at the CJHL Prospects Game's Junior A showcase in Hamilton a day later, and the draft began to feel like more of a reality than an impossibility.

He knew, though, that if he was going to be picked that it was going to be late, and if he was going to solidify his case, he'd need the OJHL playoffs to do it, especially after he'd cooled off in February, posting just four points in eight games to finish his draft year with 26 goals and 51 points in 47 games. When the season abruptly ended and the summer dragged on as he waited, he worried that he might slip through the cracks.

The Leafs' interest, however, never wavered. That September, when restrictions finally eased, Todd hosted the Elite Hockey U21 Showcase, a tournament that brought top drafted NHL prospects together with top 2020 hopefuls from the Toronto area one last time before the draft, and Leafs director of hockey and scouting operations Reid Mitchell reached out to him for video of it so that he could pass it around the office. In a rush, Todd got him the tape, knowing that Ryan had scored 16 points in six games to lead the showcase in scoring, outproducing older, already-drafted prospects like the Canucks' Ethan Keppen, Panthers' Cole Schwindt, Blues' Keean Washkurak, Hurricanes' Jamieson Rees, Devils' Graeme Clarke, and soon-to-be top 2020 picks Brennan Othmann and Francesco Pinelli.

After that tournament, the Leafs reached out to Ryan and his advisors, asking to interview him. They eventually sat down with him to get to know him a little better and go over clips they'd cut of his play, discussing with him what he did right and wrong and where he needed to improve.

Still, when his draft day rolled around, Ryan and Todd wondered whether after everything that had happened, and with just one year at the Junior A level, he'd be picked at all. He held out hope for the Leafs, who were also his and his mom's favourite team.

"I had hints that if I was going to be taken, it was going to be by them, but it was never promised," Ryan said. On the morning of the draft, he got up and went to the gym for a workout, checking in on the second- and third-round results between sets, knowing that he wouldn't be picked that high. After his workout, he returned home for a bit of a draft party, with friends and family coming and going as he waited on the couch. But one by one, the rounds passed him by.

"It was a long day. The draft ended very late, and I was just waiting around the whole day. Morale was getting lower. It was tough toward the end," Ryan said.

By the time the seventh round rolled around, and the Leafs had just two remaining picks, Ryan knew that they were likely his last shots at being selected. When the Leafs used the first of those selections, the 189th pick, to select Dexter Southfield School captain and Harvard University commit John Fusco, and their second one, 195th overall, to select Waterloo Black Hawks forward Wyatt Schingoethe out of the USHL, he thought it was over and allowed himself to be overwhelmed by the disappointment that he wasn't going to be picked.

Next to him on the couch, Todd allowed himself to feel the same way.

"We knew there was interest and we thought they were going to take him but then it's just getting so late, and these kids are getting drafted in the fifth and sixth round and it's hard as a parent not to think, 'This is just like the OHL draft.' I'm thinking, 'Ryan's got a much better future than these guys,'" Todd said. "And when they took their last pick, that was it, we thought it was over."

But in the final minutes of the draft, things took a sudden turn when the Leafs made a move, swapping their 2021 seventh-round pick for the Bruins' 2020 seventh-round pick, to acquire one last selection, 213th overall (the fifth-to-last pick of the draft). As they did it, Ryan got a phone call from the Leafs telling him they were going to use it on him.

"You get the call after waiting around all day and it goes from low to high," he said, recalling that moment. "I was just right back up."

IF THE PANDEMIC made Ryan's draft year unconventional, unanticipated, and topsy-turvy, it turned his post-draft season into something else altogether.

On October 16, a little more than a week after the draft, as the second wave of the pandemic worsened, 18 of the players on the Yale men's hockey team, who play out of Harvard's Ivy League circuit, tested positive for COVID. A few weeks later, the Ivy League cancelled its season for the second straight year, this time before it even got off the ground. When it did, the Harvard men's hockey team gave its players permission to play elsewhere (with several returning to the USHL, which played its 2020–21 season uninterrupted) or transfer schools altogether. Harvard also told Ryan that because it was going to have to push back eligibility for each player on the current roster, it would also likely be pushing back each of the upcoming recruiting classes by a year, meaning that he may not be able to join until the 2022–23 season.

Meanwhile, it also became clear that the OJHL's season would not get going, either, as it and the OHL were prevented to operate under provincial health restrictions in Ontario. Not only could Ryan not begin his college career for a further two seasons, but he also couldn't return to the Jr. Canadiens for a second campaign. Without anywhere to play, he and Todd pleaded with Jr. Canadiens general manager Blake Ricci for a move to the Junior A BCHL.

"It was kind of weird because we were very loyal to the Jr. Canadiens. Ryan has probably played there longer than every other tenured player ever, but it was clear in my mind that the OJHL wasn't going to play and the BCHL was, so we had Ryan's advisor talk to the team and so did I," Todd said. "They didn't want to trade him, of course, but we were just like, 'You've got to do it for Ryan's well-being.' And the Leafs were like, 'We'd like to see this kid play,' so we were trying to find him a spot."

After several discussions, Ricci and his staff obliged and on October 26, Ryan was traded to the Alberni Valley Bulldogs in Port Alberni, British Columbia, on Vancouver Island, for the rights to one of their players, Keaton Mastrodonato, and future considerations. Though the BCHL wasn't formally up and running, it was playing regional games and tournaments in localized areas. While it never showed up on an official stats page, Ryan began to play in his first games since February 22 of that year, a full eight months earlier. After making six appearances in the Islander Cup games played against the league's three other teams located on Vancouver Island, however, the BCHL also stopped its own season before it ever formally began.

Without a place to play for a second time in a month, Ryan and his advisors then began looking into a transfer for him. And when word got out that he may be looking to leave Harvard, Todd guesses that as many as 20 schools reached out in the first week to test his interest in a move. Among them were the four schools that he'd visited a year earlier. But Ryan didn't get a good feel from any of them, and he knew that his grades were good enough to land him wherever he wanted. (He was never the best student in the class, but he was always a good one and had been named his graduating class' valedictorian in elementary school.) Then the coaching staff at the University of Connecticut reached out and offered to bring him in right away, even though it was already several games into the NCAA's Hockey East conference schedule.

"It was a weird situation because normally the coaches will come out and watch live games, but this was the first time that they'd ever offered anybody without the head coach seeing him," Todd said.

After Ryan did some research on UConn, he and his dad made a last-minute visit to its campus in Storrs, Connecticut, and Ryan fell in love with it as soon as they pulled in.

"It was very tricky, playing junior, and COVID, and just waiting around. When stuff with Harvard got a little complicated and then I just got the chance to go right into school, it sounded like, 'Why not?'" Ryan said. "I just felt like it was something that needed to be done."

As part of his transfer, Ryan, who enrolled in UConn's sports management program, was also promised an immediate opportunity. Though he started on the fourth line in his first game, he was playing on the second line and the power play before the year was out. Given his midseason arrival and earlier-than-anticipated jump to the college level, he also played well, registering seven points and a plus-1 rating in 14 games.

"It was definitely different hopping in halfway through the year when the rest of the guys have already been there," Ryan said, "but they were great in getting me into the speed of things so that I could just try and compete, that's it. Thankfully it worked out because it was a long time coming."

WHEN RYAN PICKS up his phone in the fall of 2021 to reflect on the wild two years that preceded it, he's back on campus at UConn, in the double room that he shares with one of his teammates. And things have finally stabilized. Though it's technically his sophomore season, he's in residence as if he were one of the freshmen, going through what feels like his freshman year. After everything that happened in his first half season at UConn, he's planning to spend another four full years with the Huskies under the NCAA's new exemptions for five-year student-athletes.

It has been crazy, he says, but he feels like he's starting to thrive. It shows on the ice, too. Nine games into his sophomore year, he leads UConn in scoring with seven goals and 13 points (three more than his nearest teammate, Nashville Predators fourth-rounder and senior Jachym Kondelik). He's starting to feel like he did in those early minor hockey days again.

And he's thankful. For the Leafs, who took a chance on him. And for the support of his dad, who helped him get this far through countless hours spent on the ice together and eventually through that tape he sent the Leafs (of the tournament he organized, no less).

"My dad has been great from day one, since like 15 years ago when I first started playing, teaching me how to skate and just always being there, always watching my games, coming to as many games as he can—more than he should. He's always giving me critiques and telling me what to work on. He's like a second coach and trainer, which helped during COVID. He's the biggest part of where I am," Ryan says.

That it was the Leafs who drafted him has proven to be the biggest blessing of his life, though, he says.

These last two years, they've been his one constant.

If any other team had drafted him, he wouldn't have been able to get any face time with the team or get onto the ice with its staff. That was true for most college players, who typically return to campuses in August, even in the Before Times, let alone in the After Times of the pandemic. Because the Leafs selected him, he has spent the last two summers making daily trips from Richmond Hill to Etobicoke to skate with their informal summer group at their practice facility, the Ford Performance Centre. Ryan grew up playing in games, practices, and tournaments at the Ford Performance Centre fourplex of rinks and guesses he skated on the Leafs' pad "hundreds of times." So skating there, now as a member of the Leafs, and having access to the sliding doors that open up into the Leafs' locker room, has been something that he used to dream about, watching as the Leafs players came and went as a kid. He was even able to fit in a few more skates during UConn's two-week Christmas break in his freshman year.

"To see their little facilities down there, to be a part of that, and to see their workout room out to the side that I've never seen, it's pretty cool," he said, pausing. "It's hard to believe."

Even harder to believe, though, were the greetings of "Bergy, how's it going?" when he returned from UConn to rejoin the skates in his first full off-season as a member of the Leafs organization. He was stunned when all the players and staff remembered him from the year prior.

"It's just a very small group of like eight to 10 of us to start. So I'm just skating around, working out, and just talking with [Jason] Spezza, [Jake] Muzzin, [Zach] Hyman when he was there, and [Travis] Dermott. So that's just pretty cool, to walk around and hang out with the guys that you see on TV every night. And they're all great guys. Like you walk in there, you don't know how these guys are going to act, but everyone's just awesome and just talking to you. It's great. They're all very good people," Ryan said.

Todd has seen a change in his son, too. When Ryan returns from a skate or a game of ultimate frisbee with the Leafs, his eyes are lit up and he carries himself differently.

"It has been fantastic that the Leafs took him. So many things have opened up for him and his motivation level is just through the roof. I've never seen him like this," Todd said. "The best thing about Ryan is his competitiveness is crazy. I know a lot of people say that, but until you meet the kid and see how hard he tries, you won't get it. Even if you're just playing a stupid game that he picked up at the house for the first time, he's not messing about. He wants to win. That has helped him get a long way because in those formative years he always had to play tough because he was smaller. And ever since the Leafs selected him, it's night and day the amount of work and effort he's putting in, even compared to what he was like before. It's a new level right now."

When Ryan stops to consider his life since the start of the pandemic, his winding road to the draft and beyond, and everything else—the text messages he exchanges with Dr. Hayley Wickenheiser, the Leafs' Hockey Hall of Famer senior director of player development, the video sessions they do with him to go over his games in segments and break things down for him, all of it—he can't help but wonder what would've happened if the Leafs didn't make that last-second trade to grab him.

But they did, and they changed his life, and he made it through the other side of a two-year period that could have gone in a completely different direction, with his dream still in sight.

And that, he says, is what the draft—and his dream—is all about.

ACKNOWLEDGMENTS

IN THE DAYS after I signed on to do this book in December 2020 and began telling friends and family about it, my plans were met with chuckles, headshakes, and dropped mouths.

Not in, "That's great news and I'm shaking my head because I can't believe it!" or, "My mouth is open because I'm excited for you!" kinds of ways, but in the, "You know you're having a kid in five months, right?" kind of way. Some combination of, "You're crazy," or, "You don't know what you're getting yourself into," or, "You better get most of it done before the baby comes" usually followed.

My wife, MJ, (who was a couple months pregnant with our first child, Beaumont, when this publisher presented me with the idea that fall) reacted differently. She gave me the kind of sappy grin that only someone who really knew *me* and just how much I'd want to do something like *this* could. There was no pause to question whether I should take on my first book, while still working my job at The Athletic full-time, in the middle of a pandemic, with our first kid—and all the craziness that would (and did) come with him—on the way. There was no hesitation. She just said, "Do it." And whenever I came up with a but-but-but as I mulled it over, she just kept saying it.

"Do it. Do it. Do it. You won't regret it. We'll make it work."

But in the 11 months after I started the book and before I submitted this manuscript—and the year of editing and pagination that followed before it was published—*she* made it work a heck of a lot better than *we* did.

From December to Beaumont's birth on May 7, 2021, I spent my weekdays sitting at our kitchen table doing my work for The Athletic, and almost all my weeknights and weekends writing this book. A few days before Beaumont's due date, a pipe above our living room burst, flooding our small home and forcing us out in the middle of the night to my in-laws' place north of the city. Though Beaumont was born in Toronto, he didn't come home to it until three-and-a-half months later, once the insurance company—and its many delays—had replaced the plumbing, ceilings, and floors. Even during the seven weeks of parental leave I took from The Athletic, I spent many of those days (too many) squirreling away to the office at my in-laws' home to write the manuscript or conduct and transcribe interviews.

MJ, even when she had every right to, never said a word. Not as she navigated motherhood for the first time. Not as she sang lullabies into the wee hours, barely able to hold the weight of the baby in her arms in those first few days, carrying Beaumont around her parents' basement. Not as she shuffled Beaumont to and from the city, taking him to doctor's appointments or by our construction site to check on progress. Not when we were finally back home in Toronto and she'd stop whatever she was doing to scoop up Beaumont, take him upstairs, and close the door of his bedroom whenever she heard my phone ring because she wanted to make sure that he didn't make any noise while I was on a call for the book. Not in the home stretch, when I began to travel again for The Athletic, leaving her alone for weeklong trips to Calgary in the summer when Beaumont was still a newborn, or Traverse City in the fall as his sleep schedule changed, or Edmonton at Christmas as he learned to crawl. Not when I hit a wall in the writing process and began escaping to the nearby Riverdale Library, even when I was home, to finish the final chapters.

For each of those reasons, this book belongs to her more than me.

It also belongs to the many others who supported me—and her, and Beaumont—throughout its authoring. It belongs my parents-in-law, Heather and Andy, who took us in for 101 days (not that we were counting!) after the flood, cooking us meals and swanning in during the most difficult nights to take Beaumont for a couple of hours so that we could get some rest—and to Heather, in particular, for painting each room of our house while I worked on the book in the final months of MJ's pregnancy. It belongs to people like my brother-in-law, Michael, who repeatedly came by the house after we were back in to do odd jobs that I had neglected to get to (or, as those who know me would likely tell you, am incapable of doing). It belongs to my parents, for their unending support of MJ and me in all that we do and of me in my pursuit of this crazy career specifically—and to my mom for endowing in me some of her research skills. It belongs to my sister-in-law, Meg, who also happens to be a literary agent who helped me navigate the early stages of this process, on her own time, when I was out of my depth.

And most of all, it belongs to the many subjects who answered my calls and spoke with me for much longer, and in much greater detail, than they needed to (in almost every case on multiple occasions).

David Gregory. Walt McKechnie. Bruce Boudreau. Randy Carlyle. Bob McGill. Peter Ihnacak. Wendel Clark. Gord Stellick. Scott Thornton. Steve Bancroft. Danny Flynn. Drake Berehowsky. Todd Warriner. Staffan Kronwall. John Ferguson Jr. Luke Schenn. Dave Poulin. Chris Bergeron. Rico Blasi. Brendan Shanahan. Jack Han. Ryan and Todd Tverberg. The many others from around the sport who spoke with me off the record or connected me with the right people. And Steve Dangle, for writing the foreword with the levity and energy that only he is capable of.

These stories really belong to them, in the end. In some cases, like Wendel's, I was asking them to provide new details in stories they've told hundreds of times. In others, like with Tyler Biggs' story (which I knew would be the longest chapter of the book and the toughest to write), I was asking people to tell a story about someone else when Tyler and his father Don politely declined to speak with me for the book.

Don wrote the following back to me in a text:

Scott,

Spoke with Tyler and he has moved on with his life. The past is the past and you can't change it. People will say what they want no matter how the story is told.

Thanks for asking. Take care.

So it's not lost on me that these stories don't really belong to me. The book might, but the stories don't—at all. That much hit home for me when Bergeron, after we were done speaking for the chapter on Biggs, finished by saying, "I hope this is a celebration of Tyler more than it is negative," because his words were a clear sign of the *we*—of the humanity—at play.

I hope this book respected that *we* has its limits for me as a writer, telling stories about people who are not me, just as it did when MJ told me, "*We'll* make it work," knowing full well that *she* would need to.

Without her—and all those many others—making room for me to tell these stories, and without the people who lived them filling that room with theirs, this book never gets into your hands.

ABOUT THE AUTHOR

SCOTT WHEELER IS a national reporter with The Athletic based out of Toronto. He covers the NHL draft and prospects. He is a graduate of Carleton University's school of journalism. *On the Clock: Toronto Maple Leafs: Behind the Scenes with the Toronto Maple Leafs at the NHL Draft* is his first book.